PROTECT YOURSELF
FROM
REAL ESTATE
AND
MORTGAGE
FRAUD

Perserving the American Dream of Homeownership

Ralph R. Roberts, CRS, GRI | Rachel M. Dollar, Esq., CMB

KAPLAN

PUBLISHING

New York

This publication is designed to provide accurate and authoritative information in regard to the subject matter covered. It is sold with the understanding that the publisher is not engaged in rendering legal, accounting, or other professional service. If legal advice or other expert assistance is required, the services of a competent professional should be sought.

Editorial Director: Jennifer Farthing
Development Editor: Joshua Martino
Production Editor: Fred Urfer
Production Artist: Todd Bowman
Cover Designer: Rod Hernandez

Kaplan Publishing books are available at special quantity discounts to use for sales promotions, employee premiums, or educational purposes. Please email our Special Sales Department to order or for more information at *kaplanpublishing@kaplan.com,* or write to Kaplan Publishing, 1 Liberty Plaza, 24th Floor, New York, NY 10006.

Dedications

From Ralph: To the honest homeowners and real estate professionals who play fair and work hard to preserve the American dream of homeownership; to my wife, Kathleen; and to my kids, Kolleen (*www.KolleenRoberts.com*), Kyle, and Kaleigh

From Rachel: To my mother, E. Mary Dollar, and in memory of my father, John M. Dollar, who raised me to distinguish right from wrong in a culture of increasing moral relativism

Acknowledgments

All books are a team project, but this book more than most required a team of dedicated industry insiders, concerned antifraud activists, and victims who were courageous enough to speak out. We would like to give special thanks to our contributors, who you will meet throughout the book, including Bill Matthews, Kathy Coon, Ann Fulmer, John Jacobs, Debbie Yack, Marge Fraser, Michael Blackburn, and Ed Rybczynski.

Lois Maljak deserves a big round of applause for keeping the writing team on track, on schedule, and often, quite literally, on the same page. We would also like to thank our agent, Neil Salkind of Studio B, for believing in this book and committing himself to its success.

From Rachel: A big thank-you to Glenn Smith for reading the manuscript and for keeping me focused on writing over Christmas in Hawaii, and to Sheila Force for her input and focus. Thank you also to the readers of Mortgage Fraud Blog and all of the real estate professionals who join me in my efforts to educate consumers and professionals and eradicate mortgage fraud.

From Ralph: Thanks to all the people who have joined me in fighting the good fight against real estate and mortgage fraud: Paul Pash, former police commissioner of Warren, who reviewed thousands of files with me and helped deliver them personally to the proper authorities; Detective Darryl L. Gracey; Don Fresard, chief of staff of the Wayne County Prosecutor's Office, who has been most diligent in the fight; Howard Brinton, who realized that real estate and mortgage fraud are serious issues and who collaborated with me on the educational series "Detecting and Preventing Real Estate Fraud"; Marge Fraser, educator and owner of Real Estate School, who understands the deleterious effects of fraud on our industry and is dedicated to protecting professionals and homeowners alike; Ann Millben, licensing administrator, Michigan State Department of Consumer & Industry Services; John E. Jacobs, attorney at law; Mark Hackel, Macomb County Sheriff; Ronda Heilig, FBI, Washington, D.C.; and all of the reporters across the nation who have increased the public's awareness of real estate and mortgage fraud. Thanks also to the 200,000 readers who visit *FlippingFrenzy.com* every month, and to all of the real estate professionals who join me in my efforts to educate the world about real estate fraud every day.

The American dream of home-ownership is under siege by a growing army of con artists, misguided real estate professionals, and ill-informed homeowners who honestly believe that fudging the information on a legal document "doesn't really hurt anyone."

Together, these uninformed individuals and opportunists are chipping away at the foundation of homeownership. Their actions have fleeced homeowners and lenders out of billions of dollars, artificially inflated housing prices and property taxes, made homes less affordable and loans less accessible to honest citizens, and continue to drive homeowners into foreclosures in epidemic numbers.

According to the Federal Bureau of Investigation, real estate fraud is one of the fastest growing white-collar crimes in the United States. From 2003 to 2004, reports of mortgage fraud jumped 146 percent! From 2004 to 2005, they jumped another 28 percent, and the first quarter of 2006 reflects a 35 percent increase in reports over the same period in 2005. If the trend continues, our children and grandchildren will find the American dream of homeownership completely unattainable, and the real estate landscape will transform from a burgeoning metropolis into a ramshackle slum.

As with most crimes, the authorities alone are unable to stop real estate and mortgage fraud. As quickly as they enact a new law or a system for preventing fraud, the con artists identify another loophole or vulnerability in the system. To defend the American dream of homeownership, to protect ourselves from falling victim to real estate scams, and to avoid becoming unwitting accomplices, we have to work together to beat back the unrelenting army of con artists. We need to become well aware of the risks, be able to spot the signs of a shady deal, and have the integrity and backbone to abort and report fraudulent transactions.

Protect Yourself from Real Estate and Mortgage Fraud is your training manual. With detailed overviews of each type of real estate and mortgage fraud and compelling case studies illustrating exactly how these scams unfold, *Protect Yourself from Real Estate and Mortgage Fraud* empowers you with the information and resources you need to protect your home, family, business, and neighborhood from the ravages of fraud.

We talk to real estate professionals from around the world. Many mention that they've encountered fraudulent deals, but when we ask if they've reported them, most say no. In other words, they refuse to be a part of the fraudulent deal, but they choose not to take the next step. Very likely, the con artist simply took his scheme down the road and found a more willing accomplice. *Protect Yourself from Real Estate and Mortgage Fraud* encourages you to practice the S-T-O-P approach to shutting down fraud:

- SPOT it.
- STOP it.
- POST it (report it).

To save the American dream of homeownership, every homeowner and real estate professional must pledge allegiance to the dream and vow to act with honesty and integrity. Every real estate transaction involves a half-dozen people or more, but it takes only one individual to stop a fraudulent transaction. We want *you* to be that person—the one person at the closing table with the knowledge and integrity to make a difference. We want you to be an army of one and join our ranks as a real estate scam-buster, working to preserve the American dream and protect your home, your family, yourself, and your community.

Limit of Liability/Disclaimer of Warranty

While the publisher and authors have used their best efforts in preparing this book, they make no representations or warranties with respect to the accuracy or completeness of the contents of this book and specifically disclaim any implied warranties of merchantability or fitness for a particular purpose. No warranty may be created or extended by sales representatives or written sales materials. The advice and strategies contained herein may not be suitable for your situation and are not intended as a replacement for legal advice from a qualified attorney. This book is for general informational purposes only. Consult an attorney in your area for advice concerning your specific situation. Neither the publisher nor the authors shall be liable for any loss or damages, including but not limited to special, incidental, consequential, or other damages. An indictment is merely an accusation and all defendants are innocent until proven guilty in a court of law.

1

REAL ESTATE FRAUD:

What It Is and Why It Happens

R eal estate is a multitrillion-dollar-a-year industry. It fuels the American economy; builds personal wealth; and employs millions of mortgage bankers, real estate professionals, contractors, and others who make an honest living financing, buying, selling, and improving homes.

Unfortunately, money attracts more than homeowners, investors, and honest professionals. It also attracts thieves—people looking to score large amounts of quick cash by cheating others out of their hard-earned money. Through various clever scams and schemes, con artists have figured ways to pick the pockets of the real estate industry and individual homeowners, often with the assistance of the very professionals in the industry who stand to suffer most from the industry's demise.

In this chapter, we define *real estate fraud* and *mortgage fraud* and present a few examples of common scams. We then investigate the many manifestations of real estate fraud and uncover the driving forces that have enabled it to become such a rampant problem.

DEFINING REAL ESTATE FRAUD

Real estate fraud consists of any misrepresentation in a real estate transaction intended to cheat someone out of money or property, obtain housing under false pretenses, or secure better credit terms. Real estate fraud manifests itself in a number of ways, including the following:

- Lying on a loan application to qualify for a higher loan amount
- Charging a higher price for a house in order to absorb the down payment or provide the buyer with cash back at closing
- Convincing a homeowner facing foreclosure that the only way to save the home is to deed it to another person or entity for a year (usually with the intent of stealing the property)
- Lying about your intent to live in your investment property or second home so that you can obtain a lower interest rate on the loan
- Artificially inflating the value of a home and selling the over-priced piece of property to an unsuspecting buyer
- Seducing borrowers to sign for mortgages with low initial payments so they end up in a situation in which they will almost assuredly default on the loan
- Moving into someone's house when they're on vacation and selling it
- Renting a property and then acting as the owner and selling it

As you can see, real estate fraud covers a wide range of criminal activity. Some types of conduct are grey areas—questionable deals that fairly honest people have no trouble justifying. Other types are outright scams that anyone with a shred of moral fiber can easily distinguish as fraud.

DEFINING MORTGAGE FRAUD

Mortgage fraud is a subset of real estate fraud that deals exclusively with the misrepresentation of information in connection with obtaining a mortgage or home equity loan. Any activity or information intended to mislead the lender is mortgage fraud. This includes inflating the appraised amount of the property to borrow money in excess of the property's value, claiming that the buyer intends to live in the property when he's actually purchasing it as an investment, or claiming that an applicant is earning more money than she actually earns. In fact, most of the examples set forth under the definition of real estate fraud are actually mortgage fraud! This is because the main motivating factor in committing fraud is generally to obtain money. Because of the large dollar amounts involved in real estate transactions, a loan is usually required in order to obtain the cash to buy or sell real estate.

THREE DRIVING FORCES OF REAL ESTATE FRAUD

If you watch detective shows, you know that people end up on a list of suspects when they have the *means, motive,* and *opportunity* to commit a crime. These same three factors contribute to the rising incidence of real estate fraud, but they express themselves in ways that are unique to real estate. In the following sections, we explore these factors in greater detail to offer a general explanation of the root causes of real estate and mortgage fraud.

Means

Relatively recently, some of the tools that the real estate industry implemented to streamline the process of buying and selling homes and applying for loans have greatly simplified the task for real estate con artists. These tools include the following:

- *Impersonal transactions.* In the good old days, when you wanted to borrow money, you had to look your lender in the eye as you handed over your paperwork. Your banker was located in your community and knew information about your job, family, and financial situation. Nowadays, you can apply for a loan over the phone or on the Internet. You don't even have to be a good liar. Gone are the days of *It's a Wonderful Life*, with George Bailey fighting on behalf of the homeowner. Community has succumbed to globalization. Even if your banker is your next-door neighbor, he doesn't really know you. Lenders are often in a position of making loans to nonhumans, made-up people, or virtual beings.
- *Easy access to personal information on the Internet.* Real estate con artists often employ identity theft in their fraudulent schemes, and the Internet makes identity theft far too easy. For a small fee, you can purchase a dossier on someone, complete with name, Social Security number, credit card numbers, and other personal information that makes it easy to take on the identity of someone else.
- *Proliferation of computerized tools for faking documents.* With a small investment of about $1,000, you can buy a computer and printer combination that's quite good at faking just about any official document—from birth certificates to paycheck stubs to tax returns and even signed deeds. Even law enforcement officials sometimes have a tough time distinguishing an original from a counterfeit.
- *Demystification of the lending process and simplification of programs.* In the past, only a select group of insiders understood the process and criteria for obtaining a mortgage loan. The requirements for obtaining a mortgage loan were very specific and sometimes difficult to understand and comply with. The real estate industry now employs over nine million people and is responsible for over 20 percent of America's gross national product. Qualification criteria have been simplified and documentation requirements have been reduced. As a result, the

lending process has become more widely understood, which, while desirable, also opens the industry to abuse.

In the mid '70s, the con artists were selling properties at market value to dead people. Nowadays, they're selling properties at highly inflated prices to people who never existed. The difference now is that computers and the Internet have removed the human factor. Computers are automating the approval process, and computers are easily fooled, giving the con artists easy access to cold, hard cash.

Motive

Behind every crime is a motive. In the case of real estate fraud, the motive is usually housing or money:

- *Fraud for housing.* People who can't afford a home often resort to desperate measures—lying about their assets and income, convincing a relative to act as the buyer, obtaining phony financial documents, or hooking up with con artists to pay more for a house than what it's worth simply because they can't buy a house legitimately. A brother may cosign for a loan and claim he's going to live in the house when he has no intention of doing so. Some buyers lie to buy a more expensive house than they can afford, obtain a better interest rate on a loan, or qualify for a loan to buy investment properties or a second home.
- *Fraud for profit.* The profit motive is at the root of most theft, including real estate fraud. In fraud-for-profit schemes, the house is merely a vehicle that the con artist uses to get at the cash. In the most blatant cases, fraudsters sell a house right from under the owners or use a phony deed to convince the homeowners that they lost the house in foreclosure. In less obvious cases, the fraudsters sell a house for much more than it's worth and simply pocket the proceeds as if they had merely made a good business decision.

Erosion of **M**orality and **E**thics

People are generally ethical until they either need or want something that they can't obtain legitimately or they look around and see that the unethical crowd is winning the game of life. Then they begin to bend or break the rules. In the real estate industry, both situations are becoming increasingly common. When housing prices are on the rise and incomes aren't keeping up, people are desperate to purchase a house and often resort to fudging the facts to achieve their dream of homeownership. When they look around and see that "everyone is doing it," they justify their lies to the point at which fraud may seem perfectly legitimate.

Many drug dealers have chosen to change careers—to real estate and mortgage fraud, because they have a lower likelihood of being caught. Even if they are caught, they rarely get more than a few years in prison and often get to keep most of their ill-gotten gains. David Jackson, an investigative reporter at the *Chicago Tribune,* has documented this tragic trend in his series "The New Street Hustle." A con artist convicted of stealing tens of millions of dollars may spend 5 to 10 years in jail, but when he gets out, if he was successful in hiding the proceeds of his crime, he can look forward to a life of luxury on a warm, remote island.

Opportunity

Driven by greed and possessing the basic tools required to start churning out lies, all that stands in the way of someone willing and able to commit fraud is opportunity, and in real estate, opportunity abounds:

- *Availability of loans.* The cost of money, like the cost of just about everything, is driven by supply and demand. With low-interest mortgages available and the resulting proliferation of low-documentation loan programs, money becomes much more easily accessible to both legitimate and illegitimate borrowers. This easy access leaves the cash box wide open for con artists to reach in and help themselves.

- *Careless procedures and practices.* As competition heats up in the lending industry, commissioned real estate agents and loan officers have incentive to close more deals. Motivated to obtain a higher percentage of sales, loan officers often fail to perform their due diligence, or worse—some actually encourage homeowners to lie on their loan applications to obtain approval for a loan!

- *Delays in recording deeds and other documents.* Following every real estate transaction, the county clerk or register of deeds must record and file the paperwork to create an accurate account of the transaction. In some areas, the recording process is delayed by several weeks or even months. Real estate con artists spot this vulnerability in the system and exploit it. They can sell a property to three or four different buyers before the paperwork for the first transaction is ever recorded.

- *Desperate homebuyers.* When people are desperate, they become easy prey for scoundrels. Wanting a home so badly, they're willing to do almost anything to get it, and this desperation provides the perfect opportunity for con artists to ply their tactics.

With means, motive, and opportunity in such high supply, you might begin to think that fraud is unstoppable, but we believe that real estate and mortgage fraud can be stopped or at least significantly limited. The) first line of defense is education—of both consumers and real estate professionals. By reading this book, you are arming yourself with the education you need to become an active warrior in the fight against real estate and mortgage fraud.

HOW CAN THIS BE HAPPENING?!

Homeowners generally assume that real estate professionals are looking out for them or at least policing their industry. After all, real estate professionals have the most to lose if rampant fraud erodes the very foundation of homeownership. Unfortunately, however, some real estate professionals have been slow to respond. In fact, many in the industry actually profit from real estate and mortgage fraud in the form of increased business, higher commissions, and even proceeds from fraudulent transactions. Studies estimate that up to 80 percent of fraudulent transactions in the housing industry involve the participation of an industry insider. In many cases, the insider believes that what she's doing is perfectly legitimate.

Through this book, growing media attention, and blogs like *FlippingFrenzy.com* and *MortgageFraudBlog.com,* we hope to turn the tide on real estate and mortgage fraud by increasing awareness and education for both homeowners and real estate professionals. For specific suggestions for fixing the system to make it less vulnerable to fraud, see chapter 21.

C h a p t e r

2

FRAUD'S DEVASTATING IMPACT ON HOMEOWNERS, NEIGHBORHOODS, AND NATIONS

Real estate fraud is not a victimless crime. It impacts homeowners by artificially inflating the value of their homes and subsequently their property taxes. It makes homes less affordable for buyers, increases mortgage interest rates, bankrupts homeowners, ruins legitimate real estate businesses, and transforms neighborhoods into ghost towns. It even threatens the national economy by threatening the health and solvency of the lending industry and straining law enforcement resources.

In this chapter, we reveal real estate fraud's devastating impact on homeowners, neighborhoods, and nations in the attempt to sound the wake-up call. Until we all realize the serious threat posed by real estate fraud and become proactive in shutting it down, the con artists will continue raiding the cookie jar until the very foundation of homeownership crumbles to the ground.

HARMING HOMEOWNERS AND TAXPAYERS

Imagine yourself living next to a house that has been vandalized by real estate fraud. Over the course of a year, your property taxes have doubled because the price paid for that home was far more than it was actually worth. Then, the people living in the home, who were suckered into paying double the home's value, lose their home in foreclosure. The bank takes it over and initiates an investigation.

For months, while the lawyers, appraisers, and bank try to figure out what happened, who should pay, and who should go to jail, the house remains vacant, and the value of your house drops. Good neighbors begin to wonder if "the neighborhood is going," and they place their houses on the market, having to sell them for tens of thousands less than they were worth only a couple years ago, because prospective buyers are wondering what's going on. As prices decline, more and more of the homes are purchased by investors who place tenants in the homes—changing the neighborhood from one that was primarily made of owner-occupied homes to a neighborhood of short-term rentals. The value of your property continues to sink. You now owe more for the house than you can sell it for, and you're living in an area that's on a fast downhill track.

Real estate fraud is not a victimless crime. If you own your own home, you need to be well aware of the potentially negative effects of real estate fraud on your personal financial health and well-being, such as the following:

- *Artificially inflated property values.* Inflated appraisals, whether they're done as part of an illegal *flipping* scheme or to provide homeowners with cash back at closing, artificially inflate property values. In the short term, if you're selling your house, this may benefit you. In the long term, inflated values create a housing bubble destined to burst. (Illegal flipping schemes, described in chapter 7, typically involve buying a run-down house, investing as little as possible to make it look nice, and then selling it for much more than its true value.)

- *Deflated property values.* When homeowners can't pay their mortgages due to inflated property values and the increased property taxes, the loan default rate in a particular area often skyrockets, leading to increased foreclosures and bankruptcies, vacant properties, and a housing market crash. In many cases, homeowners have to sell for less so buyers can afford to pay inflated property taxes. In areas where flipping schemes are prevalent, homes are abandoned or rented to undesirable tenants, which depresses property values. Other types of crime typically follow, resulting in higher rates of vandalism, burglary, and murder. The increased crime rates further erode property values.

- *Increased property taxes.* When property values soar, so do property taxes. As a homeowner, you foot the bill. Property taxes based on inflated property values often remain in effect for up to a year and a half until the assessor gets around to reassessing the property.

- *Rising interest rates.* Real estate fraud is like shoplifting. The more money the con artists steal from lenders, the more those lenders have to charge in interest rates and fees to cover their losses.

- *Lost homes, broken dreams.* Victims of real estate fraud often default on the mortgage loans and face foreclosure. In the process, they can be victimized again by a con artist who, in the guise of offering to save them from foreclosure, steals the house right out from under them, leaving them with little or none of the equity they had built up in that home.

- *Increased income taxes.* Real estate fraud costs you money even if you're not a homeowner. Some estimates show that the savings and loan bailout of the 1980s cost taxpayers as much as $175 billion. When the United States (that means *us* taxpayers) gets the final tab for real estate fraud, it's going to make the savings and loan bailout look like pocket change. Real estate fraud continues to pick the pockets of taxpayers with the costs of FBI investigations, increased regulations, and increasing defaults on government-insured loans.

- *Strapped city budgets.* A single foreclosure can cost a city up to $30,000 for additional police and fire protection, the demolition of the building, and the loss of property tax revenues. Money that would otherwise be used for city services is gobbled up in the cost of fraud, further chipping away at the foundation of the community.

If a house next to you were vandalized—covered with graffiti, windows smashed out, taken over by drug dealers and other vermin—you would probably call the police and do something about it. Real estate fraud is an even more sinister form of vandalism, yet many of us are reluctant to do what's required to stop it. Even worse, many homeowners and real estate professionals join in the process of looting and pillaging with the false belief that some forms of real estate fraud are victimless crimes.

DESTROYING NEIGHBORHOODS

Real estate swindlers often work an area. They focus on one neighborhood and mine the vein until it goes dry. In Camden, New Jersey, a drug dealer ransacked a neighborhood with a house flipping scheme he concocted with friends and family.

The crime ring consisted of a drug wholesaler and four coconspirators who used the proceeds from the dealer's crack cocaine business to buy homes, perform cosmetic property makeovers, and sell the properties to naïve buyers. In all, they purchased at least 25 homes and sold them for a total profit in excess of $1 million. The illegal house flipping ring consisted of the following players:

- The drug dealer
- The drug dealer's girlfriend, a licensed real estate agent
- The drug dealer's father, a city maintenance worker
- The girlfriend's mother, a crossing guard
- A handyman and owner of a construction business

These con artists purchased cheap, dilapidated properties, and then recruited desperate homeowner wannabes (naïve, sometimes illiterate or mentally ill individuals) to take out loans to buy the homes. The flippers produced their own phony paperwork to qualify the buyers for the loans, including fake pay stubs and employment records, W-2 forms, federal tax returns, and credit reports. They even used fake names and Social Security numbers to manufacture identities.

In lieu of cash for home repairs and renovations, the handyman accepted crack cocaine as payment and paid his workers in the same currency. The renovations were designed simply to make the houses look livable. Repairs merely hid structural defects, plumbing and electrical deficiencies, and other serious problems.

The people who bought the houses usually had to move out in a month or two, because the homes were uninhabitable. The homeowners got stuck with mortgages they couldn't afford on homes they couldn't live in. The lenders were duped out of hundreds of thousands of dollars, and because most of the mortgages were in the form of government-insured loans, the government (i.e., the taxpayers) paid the rest.

Fortunately, the ringleader was caught, convicted, and sentenced to 30 years in prison. His father received 5 years of probation.

The negative effects of real estate fraud often ripple through an area, driving the best residents out and creating a vacuum in which the criminal element moves in. Fraud destroys more than just the housing market. It destroys communities, schools, parks, and area businesses. It can literally transform a thriving town into a ghost town in a matter of months.

FUNDING DRUG TRADE, TERRORISM, AND OTHER CRIMES

In the past, mobsters and members of syndicate crime organizations often set up businesses to launder their money. They had construction companies, concrete companies, dry cleaners, and other legitimate businesses, and they processed the proceeds of their

Spotting the Signs

We asked Ann Fulmer, cofounder of the Georgia Real Estate Fraud Prevention and Awareness Coalition (GREFPAC) and vice president of Interthinx, a leading provider of fraud prevention products to the mortgage industry, to describe some of the telltale signs that mortgage fraud has afflicted a neighborhood. The signs that Ann noticed in her neighborhood show you what to watch out for in yours. Ann remembers:

"In 1996, before we even knew what mortgage fraud was, I noticed some strange people moving into the neighborhood . . . people who would either run away or stay silent when neighbors introduced themselves and asked for their new neighbors' names. People who moved into $500,000 houses but drove '84 Celicas that either had paper temporary license plates or plates that were switched from vehicle to vehicle. People who always backed their cars into the driveway and who blacked out the windows in their garages. People who moved into very exclusive, elegant homes in the middle of the night with no furniture and with all of their clothes stuffed in plastic garbage bags. And then there was the house where the new owners paid almost $300,000 too much. No one ever moved in, but UPS regularly delivered packages to the front door, packages that were picked up in the middle of the night by mysterious people who stopped only long enough to grab the boxes. Or the house with the blacked out windows that emitted very strong chemical odors after dark. These were what the FBI would call 'clues.'"

Ann and her neighbors decided to fight back. Joining forces with law enforcement agencies and local real estate professionals, they reclaimed their neighborhood and evicted the criminals. GREFPAC and its members continue to work on the local, state, and national level to increase awareness of mortgage fraud as a safety issue and help other neighborhoods reclaim their turf when mortgage fraud damages their communities. Visit GREFPAC online at *www.grefpac.org* to learn more.

criminal activities through their legitimate businesses. The laundering operation made it more challenging for law enforcement agents to trace the money back to illegal activities.

The current money laundering method of choice is real estate. Drug dealers in increasing numbers are buying and selling real estate not only to launder their money but also to generate revenue to fund their illegal activities. In many cases, even if the perpetrator is captured and convicted, he retains possession of his real estate property and gets to keep the proceeds after he's released—typically in a few years' time.

Although no publicized cases have involved the proceeds of real estate fraud being used directly to fund terrorist activities, several suspected terrorists have been convicted on mortgage fraud–related charges, and federal law enforcement agencies remain vigilant. We know that real estate fraud accounts for billions of dollars in losses annually. Because it is often difficult to trace these funds, especially after they leave the United States, law enforcement officials often can't tell where that money is going or what it is being used for.

Real estate con artists are not particular. They prey on neighborhoods with $50,000 homes. They prey on areas with $3 million homes. They work any location where they can make a quick buck conning the residents and lenders, and in real estate, that pretty much covers every neighborhood in the United States and in most other countries. No matter where you live, you and your neighbors need to remain on guard.

CASE STUDY

In Seattle, Washington, on August 9, 2006, Todd Love, 48, pled guilty in the U.S. District Court in Seattle to conspiracy to engage in money laundering. Love, who was a mortgage broker at Seattle Mortgage Advisors LLC, admitted that he assisted three drug dealers with investments in property, knowing that the hundreds of thousands of dollars in cash used as the down payments were the proceeds of illegal drug dealing. Love faces up to 20 years in prison and agreed to forfeit $149,500 in cash as part of a $600,000 forfeiture.

Protect **Y**our **N**eighborhood

It takes only one real estate con artist or team to ruin a neighborhood, but it takes the entire neighborhood to protect itself against the threat. Unfortunately, neighbors are not considered direct victims by authorities, and a neighborhood doesn't have a recognized basis to file claims seeking damages to the neighborhood. This was all too apparent in a case in which the court denied criminal restitution to a neighborhood agency that claimed a right to restitution due to the decrease in value and cost of cleaning up the area after a flipping scheme ravished the neighborhood.

You and your neighbors can, however, enforce some grassroots preventive strategies:

- Keep an eye on new people moving into your neighborhood. When real estate fraud moves in, you often notice that the people buying or renting the homes involved in the scam aren't quite on the same level, economically speaking, as the rest of the residents. These people may be victims or participants in the scheme.

- Watch for spikes in home prices. When area homes begin to sell for tens or hundreds of thousands of dollars above market value or above the initial listing price, prices are likely being artificially inflated.

- If neighbors are hospitalized or take extended vacations, watch out for transfer of title to their homes or other people moving in. Always have a number you can call to contact your neighbors if you notice suspicious activity.

- Report your suspicions to local, state, and federal authorities. See the appendix at the back of this book for contact information.

- Know your neighbors and share information with them. A neighborhood crime watch program can be very effective.

- If you notice abandoned property in your neighborhood, call a neighborhood meeting and draw up a plan to investigate what's going on with that property. Call your local police department to keep an eye on the vacant property until you can gather more information.

According to the plea agreement, in September 2003, convicted drug kingpin Robert Kesling purchased a home for $722,869. Love served as mortgage broker on the transaction. Kesling gave Love

$176,600 in cash for the down payment on the home. Love knew that Kesling made his income leading a drug organization that smuggled marijuana into the United States from Canada and cocaine into Canada from the United States. To assist Kesling in hiding the origin of the money, Love had escrow agent and attorney Joel Manalang place the funds in his escrow account. Love created false documents indicating that the money was a gift to Kesling from his father. Love also created a letter from a local accounting firm claiming that Kesling was in the property management business, and falsely indicated the firm had done his taxes for three years.

In a second transaction detailed in the plea agreement, Love assisted another accused drug dealer, Bernard R. Casey. Casey was an alleged drug dealer who worked under Joshua Macke. Macke replaced Kesling in the drug organization following Kesling's arrest. In August 2005, Casey wanted to invest some of his drug proceeds in property. Love had Manalang purchase a cashier's check for $50,485.70 to use as the down payment on some water view lots in Tacoma, Washington. Love created false documents alleging Casey was employed as vice president of Field Sales at Seattle Video Conference Center. Love's mother worked at the business and would falsely verify employment.

Finally, in a third transaction, Love took several hundred thousand dollars in cash from Macke for future property investments. Love provided the cash to Manalang asking that it be placed in the escrow account. Fearing IRS scrutiny, Manalang did not deposit the cash. Love asked for $50,000 from the cache, which he then spent for his own expenses, knowing it was the proceeds of drug trafficking.

Manalang pled guilty to money laundering and was sentenced to 18 months in prison, followed by 2 years of supervised release. Kesling pled guilty to conspiracy to distribute cocaine and marijuana and was sentenced to 17 years in prison. Casey was indicted on charges of conspiracy to distribute marijuana and conspiracy to engage in money laundering. Macke was indicted on charges of conspiracy to import marijuana, conspiracy to distribute cocaine and marijuana, and conspiracy to engage in money laundering. Both Casey and Macke are currently scheduled to be tried in April 2007.

Insights from an **Ex-C**on

Prior to his conviction, Baltimore, Maryland's Ed Rybczynski was a licensed title agent and the owner of a successful title company. Nowadays, during his presentations, Rybczynski speaks candidly about his role in a well-publicized flipping scheme that resulted in his serving time in a federal prison. Rybczynski's message is a simple one: Real estate fraud prevention can only be accomplished through personal accountability and responsible corporate citizenship. In other words, everyone involved in the transaction of buying and selling a house needs to realize the pain and damage that fraud inflicts on real people.

According to Rybczynski:

"Real estate—related crime is still perceived as being benign and victimless. It's not true; every aspect of our society suffers when a home is foreclosed and a family displaced. We've all heard the catchphrases: 'No one will know!' 'Everybody gets paid!' 'What difference does it make? The buyer still gets the house!'

"Awareness is the key. Through training, real estate professionals must be exposed to the possible consequences of their professional decisions. They must learn that an over-inflated appraisal or falsified bank verification can cause real harm (and pain) to children, families, and communities. Additionally, real estate professionals must be exposed to the personal consequences of improper behavior including the payment of restitution, incarceration, the loss of a career, and the loss of professional legitimacy. Then will title agents and loan brokers fully recognize the need to develop a decision-making model based on core values. Then, and only then, will mortgage fraud statistics begin to decline. Remember, mortgage fraud cannot exist without the participation of real estate professionals."

3

PLAYER PROFILES:

Who's In on It? Who Can Fix It?

Real estate fraud is a team sport. Although a ringleader often throws the opening pitch, executing the scam typically requires a team of coconspirators, including a homebuyer or homeseller and one or more of the following: listing agent, selling agent, REO (real estate owned) broker, mortgage broker, loan officer, appraiser, notary, title company, closing agent, or attorney. Further contributing to the problem are Web-based companies that facilitate fraud by offering fake documents, novelty pay stubs, rentable assets, credit enhancement, and other items that can make borrowers look good on paper. Late-night TV real estate investment gurus and those who stage bogus real estate investment seminars add fuel to the fire by pushing their overblown promises of quick cash in real estate.

In this chapter, we present a complete roster of those who can potentially become involved in real estate fraud, describing the roles they play in legitimate transactions and how they contribute to fraud when they decide to join the dark side. This chapter also introduces the people who are responsible for fixing the system and busting the bad guys, including real estate professionals, local law enforcement agencies, county sheriffs and prosecutors, state attorney generals, the U.S. attorney general, county recorders, the Federal Bureau of Investigation (FBI), the secret service, media whistle-blowers, senators, governors, regulators, and every homeseller, homebuyer, and homeowner.

REAL ESTATE FRAUD ROSTER

In the following sections, we define each person's role in the real estate transaction process and reveal areas that are vulnerable to fraud. We are in no way implicating the huge majority of honest professionals and homeowners. Most who are involved in real estate transactions rarely commit fraud intentionally, but by knowing the role that each person plays, you can more readily spot fraud when you're close enough to witness it. In addition, this roster provides guidelines for acting ethically no matter what role you play at the closing table.

Ringleaders

Ringleaders are the worst of the bunch. These guys and gals are out for profit, pure and simple. They're the masterminds who spot the loopholes in the law and the vulnerabilities in the system and figure out ways to exploit them. Then they round up coconspirators to do the dirty work. In some cases, the ringleader is a real estate professional, but in most cases is completely independent. He usually rakes in most of the money and assumes the least amount of risk, preferring to remain in the background and keep his name from appearing on any documents.

Recruiters

Ringleaders often employ recruiters whose job it is to locate *straw buyers,* or "investors," for the ringleader's scheme. (A straw buyer is someone who signs for a mortgage on a home that they have no intention of owning or making payments toward.) Recruiters often target groups of people who are related by ethnicity, religion, or other shared characteristics or common interests. The recruiter infiltrates a group and then sells potential victims on the lure of easy cash.

Throughout this book, we reveal the many ways that recruiters ply their trade to dupe buyers, sellers, lenders, and everyone else they can con into going along with the ringleader's illegal quick-cash schemes. For now, just keep in mind that if something sounds too good to be true, it probably is.

Appraisers

The role of the appraiser is to provide an unbiased estimate of the property's market value. Inflated appraisals, as explained in chapter 4, are at the root of many real estate scams. In the following sections, we distinguish between ethical and unethical appraisers.

Ethical appraiser. An ethical appraiser ensures that everyone involved in the real estate transaction has a pretty accurate idea of the property's true market value. In this capacity, the appraiser ideally does the following:

- Provides bankers, brokers, and buyers with an unbiased valuation of the property, so they can determine for themselves whether it is a sound investment
- Informs the lender whether the property is valuable enough as collateral to cover the mortgage, so the lender can accurately assess the risk of approving the loan
- Provides any information available regarding the location or condition of the property that might affect its value

Unethical appraiser. Appraisers have a tremendous amount of power in real estate transactions because their documented opinion controls the amount of money a lender will agree to loan a buyer. Appraisers can participate in the fraud in the following ways:

- Working with the seller to artificially inflate the value of the property so that the seller can obtain a higher sales price
- Working with the buyer to artificially inflate the value of the property to obtain cash back at closing
- Hiding the true market value of the property from the lender
- Giving in to pressure from real estate agents or loan officers to inflate property values
- Failing to disclose that the property has been damaged or requires significant repairs
- Manipulating the information that is provided to the lender to conceal aspects of the property that would otherwise affect the property's value—for instance, taking photographs from an angle that hides the existence of a municipal water supply tank immediately adjacent to the property

Buyers

An ethical buyer purchases a home above board, tells the truth on her loan application, and profits at the time of purchase only by becoming the owner of a property that is likely to increase in value through natural appreciation over time. Both ethical and unethical buyers, however, can contribute to real estate fraud, as the following sections explain.

Ethical buyers. Ethical buyers often become victims or unwitting accomplices to real estate and mortgage fraud due to ignorance. As uninformed buyers, they may do the following:

- Sign a loan application that contains false information, either knowingly or unknowingly
- Allow a real estate agent, loan officer, or closing attorney to act on their behalf without reviewing documents themselves
- Allow a purchase price to be inflated to make it appear as if they contributed a down payment because they couldn't afford to make one

- Use a relative's good credit to apply for a loan, claiming that the relative will live in the property even though this relative will not be residing there
- Fudge information on a loan application because they think it is perfectly acceptable to do so or because the loan officer said it was okay

Unethical buyers. Unethical buyers are those who knowingly commit fraud to obtain housing or are motivated by promises of profit. As coconspirators in fraud, they may do the following:

- Have knowledge of real estate and finance and be involved solely for financial gain
- Function as straw buyers (Some straw buyers have no idea that what they're doing is wrong. Others know full well that they're breaking the law.)
- Structure a real estate transaction so that they obtain cash back at closing or part of the proceeds of an inflated price
- Accept money to allow another person to use their credit to obtain a mortgage (this is also referred to as acting as a straw buyer.)
- Allow a mortgage to be taken out in their name in order to help out a friend, family member, or business associate

Sellers

An ethical seller sells a home near its true market value and seeks to profit only from the sale of the home, not from any additional kickbacks or "gifts." Both ethical and unethical sellers, however, can contribute to real estate fraud, as the following sections explain.

Ethical sellers. Naïve sellers typically become unwitting accomplices to fraud through such actions as the following:

Should I Let Someone Use My Credit?

Have you ever seen an ad on eBay or Craig's List or in the local newspaper seeking "investors" to purchase property? The people who place many of these ads are actually looking for straw buyers or "straw borrowers." Essentially, the person or company running the ad offers payment, sometimes $5,000 to $10,000, to anyone willing to take out a loan (in name only) to buy property. The name of the straw buyer (straw man or "nominee") appears on the title and on the mortgage recorded against the home, but the real owner or buyer is responsible for making the loan payments. In such arrangements, the straw buyer can make a pocketful of cash in exchange for the use of his name and his ability to qualify for a mortgage loan.

Some of these offers are just scams, and the real buyers are engaging in illegal flipping or other fraudulent schemes. After collecting the proceeds from the scam, they walk away, leaving the straw buyer with payments that the straw buyer never intended to make.

In other cases, the real owners intend to make money on the properties and are just unable to obtain the loans themselves. In these cases, when the economy is rising and the real owners can flip the properties for a profit, the straw buyer suffers no actual loss. When the housing market is in a slump or the real owners can't rent or sell the properties for the amount owed, however, they just stop making payments.

When the real buyer defaults on the loan, the straw buyer is left trying to argue to the lender that they never owned the property and are not obligated to make the payments. Although the argument is somewhat logical, it doesn't hold up in court. The fact is that the straw buyer, intentionally or not, provided false information, leading the lender to believe that the straw buyer was the real borrower—the person who would be making the mortgage payments. The straw buyer (or straw borrower) participated in a scheme to trick the lender into approving a risky loan that the lender would probably not have approved knowing the facts. Although straw buyers usually claim that they were defrauded, the truth is that they perpetrated a fraud on the lender and might even face criminal prosecution!

In short, the answer to the question "Should I let someone use my credit?" is "No."

- Increasing the sales price of the house on the contracts and closing documents to provide cash back at closing to buyers who claim to want the money to cover the cost of repairs or renovations

- Attempting to obtain bank approval for a short sale (sale of the property for less than the amount owed on the loans) and allowing a sales agent to perform certain acts, such as placing items with noxious odors in the attic, to make the property appraise for less

Unethical sellers. Sellers may knowingly become the beneficiaries of fraud by seeking to profit from the sale of their home in excess of the fair market equity by doing the following:

- Flipping the house illegally to sell it at an inflated price (See chapter 7 for more about illegal flipping.)
- Functioning as a straw buyer, taking title only to later pass the house along to another person
- Agreeing to a *silent second*—a second mortgage that is not disclosed to the senior lender (the lender who holds the first mortgage). Silent seconds are typically used to disguise the fact that the buyer is not actually making a down payment but is instead borrowing the down payment from the seller.

Listing Agents

Like everyone else, listing agents can be good or bad, ethical or unethical, as described in the following sections.

Ethical listing agents. The role of the listing agent is to place the property on the market and sell it at or near market value to the buyer who offers the highest price. An ethical listing agent follows these common guidelines:

- Lists the property with local multiple listing services to make the listing publicly accessible
- Represents the seller's interests
- Remains vigilant for any signs of fraud
- Stops and reports any suspicion of fraud

Unethical listing agents. An unethical listing agent may become an accomplice to real estate fraud through the following practices:

- Agreeing not to list the property with local multiple listing services and agreeing to hide the details of the price and transaction
- Inflating the listing price to enable a cash back at closing arrangement or to facilitate some other type of fraud
- Accepting higher commissions or "gifts" as compensation for cooperation
- Altering the transaction details in the multiple listing service after the closing in order to disguise fraud
- Pressuring the appraiser to inflate the value of the home

Buyer Agents

Buyer agents are supposed to represent homebuyers in real estate transactions, and they usually do a great job at it, but they also can be seduced by the lure of quick cash. In the following sections, we distinguish between ethical and unethical buyer agents.

Ethical buyer agents. Ethical buyer agents often protect buyers from real estate marauders and assist buyers in the following ways:

- Locating homes that fit the buyers' needs and are within the price range they can afford
- Evaluating the property
- Negotiating price and terms
- Assisting buyers in applying for loans
- Facilitating home inspections

Unethical buyer agents. When buyer agents go bad, they can leave their clients with a terrible mess. Clients typically trust their agents, so when an agent is not working in the clients' best interest, clients become easy prey. Unethical buyer agents are often guilty of the following types of fraudulent practices:

- Helping the buyer fabricate information
- Collaborating with illegal house flippers to convince the buyer to purchase an overpriced property
- Encouraging the buyer to pay more for a property to obtain cash back at closing for repairs, renovations, or other expenses
- Representing the sellers' interests instead of the buyers' interests
- Refraining from trying to negotiate the sales price down to ensure a higher commission

REO Brokers

REO (real estate owned) brokers list houses that banks and other lending institutions have foreclosed on and are trying to sell. Because REO brokers have control over the listings, they have the power to influence who purchases the properties.

Ethical REO brokers. Ethical REO brokers provide fair access to the properties they list. An ethical REO broker does the following:

- Lists all properties on the multiple listing service
- Sells to anyone, not just an insider group
- Sets a fair price for the properties
- Actively markets REO properties and obtains the highest possible price for the bank or other lending institution

Unethical REO brokers. Unethical REO brokers provide an unfair advantage to the people with whom they deal. They may do the following:

- Sell to a group of select insiders, usually other real estate agents or brokers

- Not list some of their properties in the multiple listing service
- Sell properties far below market value, thereby negatively affecting neighborhood home values

Notaries

The notary is one of the few human stopgaps we have in this age when official documents are so easy to counterfeit. The notary is charged with ensuring that the person signing the official document is really the person she says she is.

Ethical notaries. Most notaries are ethical individuals, committed to preventing fraud. In this capacity, they do the following:

- Identify the signer either from personal knowledge or satisfactory evidence, such as a driver's license or state I.D. card
- Review the document being notarized to make sure it has no blank spaces that can be filled in with false information later
- Make sure the signer actually signs the document in the notary's presence
- Ensure that the person signing the document is competent and has the capacity to contract (for example, the person is not a minor, is of sound mind, and appears to understand the contract or transaction)
- Complete the notarial certificate, which might include the date of signing, notary name, expiration date of commission, and "Acting in the County of _____." (The exact language and requirements for the certificate vary by state.)

(The obligations of a notary are governed by the law of the state in which the notary is licensed.)

Unethical notaries. Some individuals entrusted to be notaries either intentionally commit fraud to benefit someone they know or do so unintentionally by not performing their duties diligently. An unethical or careless notary may do the following:

- Does not verify the signer's name against his identification, such as a driver's license
- Does not check the signature on the document against the signer's signature on other official documents or identification
- Overlooks blank spaces that must be filled in prior to signing
- Allows a person to sign who clearly doesn't know what they are doing or what they are signing

Michigan and some other states have made fraud easier by eliminating the requirement for a witness at the time of signing and notarizing a document. California, on the other hand, requires that a notary obtain the thumbprint of the signer of real estate documents, thereby reducing fraud in real estate transactions.

Loan Officers

Loan officers provide buyers with the assistance they need to obtain financing to purchase a home. Most loan officers are highly qualified professionals committed to honesty and customer service, but because they're in charge of helping buyers qualify for loans, they sometimes become participants in fraud.

Ethical loan officers. Ethical loan officers attempt to help their clients obtain loans from banks and other lending institutions. In this capacity, they do the following:

- Help the buyer determine how much she can borrow
- Assist the buyer in filling out the loan application accurately and completely
- Gather factual information and turn it over to the lender

- Assist with gathering documents to support the loan application, including verifying the buyer's employment, income, and assets
- Obtain an accurate appraisal of the property to protect both the buyer and the lender

Unethical loan officers. When loan officers become involved in fraud, they can be unwitting accomplices or mastermind the scheme. Whatever the motivation, the unethical loan officer may do the following:

- Does whatever it takes to get the mortgage approved, even if the applicant doesn't qualify
- Recommends a loan to a buyer that is not the best loan that the buyer could qualify for in order to obtain a higher commission
- Alters the VOD (verification of deposit) or VOE (verification of employment)
- Misrepresents the purpose of the loan to acquire better financing; for example, claiming the property will be used as a primary residence rather than as an investment
- Creates or alters documents to qualify borrowers for loans; for instance, pay stubs, W-2's, and bank statements
- Pressures appraisers to hide details of the property or inflate the value of the property in order to make deals work
- Creates companies to receive money from the loan to pad commissions or divert fraudulent proceeds

Independent mortgage brokerages became prevalent in the 1980s. Prior to that time, few mortgage companies existed. If you wanted to buy a home and didn't have the cash, you had to head down to your local bank or credit union to apply for a loan. Now, some unethical mortgage companies use any means possible to induce a homeowner into taking out a high-interest loan.

L *o a n* **S** *h a r k s*

As a group, loan officers are the number one active, knowing participants in mortgage fraud schemes, and most of them aren't getting pressured into it by the need to "meet quotas." Loan officers are generally commissioned agents who stand to make huge sums of money by convincing borrowers into taking out loans with higher interest rates than they would otherwise qualify for. In exchange for the loan officer's fine work, the lender pays the mortgage broker a premium.

Title Underwriters

We have never seen a case involving an unethical title underwriter. Title underwriters are the companies that actually insure the title and are large, national companies. Title underwriters are often the victim of fraud or end up paying losses associated with fraud, but because they insure the title's accuracy and don't generally have any active role in the closing of the loan, they have little to no motive or opportunity to commit fraud. Title underwriters issue "closing protection letters" through which they are sometimes held responsible for damages incurred by lenders or borrowers when a title company or closing agent commits fraud during the closing or fails to follow escrow instructions.

Title Companies

Title companies, also known as abstractors or escrow companies, often place their business on the line when they provide title work for a particular property, so they're often highly motivated to prevent fraud. Even so, title companies often assume the duties associated with closing the sales transaction and sometimes have closing agents or others who are lured by the promise of profit to commit fraud.

Ethical title companies. Ethical title companies are committed to providing buyers, sellers, and lenders with accurate information at the closing. An ethical title company will do the following:

- Thoroughly investigate the title for liens, judgments, and other defects, and report these accurately to the lender and buyer
- Prepare accurate HUD-1 (the department of Housing and Urban Development) Settlement Statements that reflect true figures from the transaction and forward them to the lenders, buyers, and sellers

Unethical title companies. Unethical title companies or closing agents may facilitate fraud by doing the following:

- Ignoring evidence of forgeries or fraud
- Falsifying chains of title or vesting statements to make it appear as if the person selling the property has owned it for longer than they actually have
- Providing inaccurate information on HUD-1 Settlement Statements. In some cases, the title company may create two different settlement statements—one for the borrower and one for the lender—to hide the true facts and figures from the lender. The HUD-1 Settlement Statement is intended to disclose all information about the closing to all parties at the closing table. Unfortunately, fraudsters have figured out a way to create two sets of HUD statements—one for the closing table and another sent to the lender that's full of misinformation.

You can usually spot the warning signs of a crooked title company at work when the broker fees (commission) are calculated on an amount other than the loan or sales amount, or if the numbers in the HUD-1 Settlement Statement don't add up.

CASE STUDY

Ed Rybczynski, the former title company owner first introduced in chapter 2, has firsthand knowledge of the pressures that often lead title companies and their agents to commit fraud. Rybczynski relates:

"On one occasion, a loan officer I knew and did business with submitted a number of orders for title work. The orders were rushed and involved the purchase of rental properties by two investors. I was assured that the investors had strong financials and that the closings would definitely take place. Expecting to close, I ordered titles and prepared title commitments. The total expense for title work, copies, judgments, lien sheets, and surveys was about $2,000. Several months passed and there was no indication that the lender was ready to move forward.

"Eventually, the loan officer explained that the deals were structured creatively, allowing the buyers to cash out at the settlement table. Because we knew each other, he confided in me. In the case of loan fraud, the bad guys have to feel the good guys out to see how far they will go. The dialog has to start somewhere. He knew that any title company would be unable to readily absorb a $2,000 loss. I was instructed to misrepresent ownership in Schedule 'A' of the title commitments to coincide with the information contained in make-believe contracts. I was forced to decide between facilitating a number of illegal flips or losing a sizable amount of money.

"In this case, I demanded and received payment for expenses. A family member of one of the investors delivered a check. It later came to light that another title company closed the deals. Obviously, my decision resulted in the loss of a source of business. I found that acting ethically (properly) can come at a high price."

Closing Officers

The closing officer typically works for the title company. She's the person who sits at the head of the table and passes the closing papers around for signature. Although most closing officers are highly qualified professionals, because they have so much power at the closing table, they're susceptible to being seduced by fraud.

Ethical closing officers. The closing officer's job is to represent the title company and to protect the title company and title underwriter, who carries the most risk. An ethical closing officer's responsibilities include the following:

- Ensuring all legal documents are accurate and in order
- Verifying that the people signing the documents are who they say they are
- Ensuring that all official documents have the appropriate signatures
- Explaining the documents and the process to the borrower, as necessary
- Disbursing funds as directed by the parties and approved by the lender
- Preparing and executing an accurate HUD-1 Settlement Statement that identifies the recipients of the money and amounts of the payments

Unethical closing officers. An unethical closing officer shows little concern for the title company or the underwriter, choosing instead to work for the con artist. The unethical closing officer will do the following:

- Overlook obvious discrepancies in the paperwork
- Look the other way when an obviously fraudulent transaction is occurring

- Benefit in some way from the fraudulent transaction, either by keeping her job or receiving some illegal payment
- Pay money out of the transaction to third parties who do not have liens against the property
- Structure closing documents to disguise cash back at closing arrangements
- Fail to pay off the liens against the property and use the money for other purposes
- Close two purchase transactions for the same property simultaneously, using the lender's money from the second transaction to pay for the purchase of the property in the first transaction—also known in the industry as a "simultaneous" or "concurrent" closing. Those closing agents who agree to handle transactions in this way are referred to as "friendly" closers.
- Close multiple owner-occupied transactions to the same buyer in a short period of time

If someone is directing you to use a specific title company and you have some concerns or suspicions about a particular deal, the closing officer or title company may be in on the scheme. The closing officer is the last line of defense for the title underwriter and the lender.

Attorneys

Sworn to uphold the law, most attorneys avoid fraud, but they may represent con artists or make recommendations to their clients based on misinformation. We often talk to homeowners and investors who've been directed by their attorneys that a particular practice is legal when it is obviously illegal. The situation occurs frequently with cash back at closing deals. Attorneys also often act as closing agents and are sometimes personally involved in fraudulent schemes themselves.

To protect yourself from inaccurate advice, seek an attorney who has a strong background in real estate law and was recommended by someone you trust. Although attorneys are often perceived as being very expensive, a good real estate attorney can provide valuable advice and help both homeowners and real estate professionals to avoid fraudulent schemes—either as a victim or a conspirator.

Real Estate Investment Gurus

Real estate investment gurus aren't all bad. The good ones tell you that investing in real estate, like anything else, is risky. They tell you that achieving success requires knowledge, hard work, and determination.

The real estate gurus who cause the most harm are those who present real estate investing as the superhighway to easy profits. These are the gurus on late-night TV and on the Internet who promise thousands of dollars a week in profits and show 30-year-old couples retired and living on some lush Caribbean island as a result of following their program. Some real estate investment gurus also travel around the country giving "free" seminars on how to profit by buying and selling probate properties or foreclosures. Others charge thousands of dollars for their advice. They boast about making easy money just so they can sell their books, tapes, and CDs.

As soon as the guru leaves town, local attorneys and real estate agents often receive a spike in phone calls from people who've lost tens of thousands of dollars following the guru's advice. In some cases, the guru's advice was simply overhyped and risky. In other cases, it was downright illegal.

Some of these gurus are actually ringleaders or recruiters who approach participants after the seminars offering to assist in locating and purchasing investment properties. These properties were often purchased by the gurus for little to nothing and are sold to the investors for far more than their actual values. In these cases, the guru uses the seminars as a method of identifying targets and makes his money by defrauding the seminar participants. Always consult a real estate attorney before you buy into some quick-cash program.

Web-based Facilitators

The Web is a black-market paradise for counterfeit documents. You can find websites open 24/7 selling everything from phony paycheck stubs and other people's personal identification information to fake deeds and anything else you might need to con someone. Here are some of the services that Web-based facilitators offer:

- *Asset rental.* If you don't own enough valuable assets to qualify for a loan, you can rent them. Asset rental can make you look like you own homes, businesses, cars, boats, and other pricey items. You don't actually own the assets, but the paper trail makes it look like you do.
- *Novelty pay stubs.* Sold as innocent "joke" items to enable you to pass yourself off as earning hundreds of thousands of dollars a year working for a major corporation, novelty pay stubs are often used to verify phony employment and income.
- *Credit enhancement.* Some Web-based facilitators offer to boost your credit score and your ability to qualify for a loan by selling you someone else's good credit. All you have to do is get your name added to someone's account who has a high credit score, and voila, your credit score jumps.
- *Fake address.* Want to avoid detection and have the police chasing a ghost? You can go online and set up a phony residential address. You can even have your mail delivered there and forwarded to you.

CASE STUDY

Fraudulent real estate transactions often involve multiple parties, each of whom participates and benefits on a different level. This case study reveals a transaction that involved sophisticated buyers, a sophisticated seller, an unethical listing agent, and a ringleader (a crooked real estate agent). Here's how the deal went down:

1. The listing agent originally listed the property for $1,850,000, which was close to its market value.
2. The ringleader found sophisticated buyers (a married couple) willing to purchase the property for $3,500,000. That's $1,650,000 more than the original asking price. For his service, the ringleader was charging 25 percent.
3. The ringleader instructed the listing agent to raise the price to $3,500,000 and write up the purchase agreement to reflect that price.

The agent representing the buyers was working for a real estate broker who was well schooled on issues dealing with real estate and mortgage fraud. When the broker noticed the huge change in the listing price, he decided to give the buyers a call. Here's an edited transcript of the conversation that the broker taped and later passed along to the FBI (names have been changed):

> **Broker:** You're working with FlimFlam Realty to buy the house on DowRidge?
>
> **Sue (one of the buyers):** Yes. We're buying it as an investment property.
>
> **Broker:** After looking at the numbers, I see that you're going to get a lot of money back at closing, right?
>
> **Sue:** Uh huh.
>
> **Broker:** How much money are you getting back at closing?
>
> **Dan (other buyer):** Well, you know, to tell you the truth, I'm an investor, okay, and I have some associates who are putting the deal together . . . they put this deal together and then they came to us to okay it.
>
> **Broker:** So these associates are going to give you something like $1 million back at closing?
>
> **Dan:** Yeah, something to that effect. Not quite that much by the time they work out the closing costs and the like . . . . Like I said, we're just the investors.

Broker: You realize that this sort of deal is fraud?

Dan: Well . . . no . . . I'll have to check that out. The deal seemed okay to us. I mean, we were going to borrow extra so we'd have money to renovate the place. The people who put this together would get 25 percent.

Broker: Why do you have to give someone 25 percent of the money?

Dan: Well, they're doing a lot of the work. They put the deal together.

To give the buyers some credit, they came clean about the transaction and cooperated in the investigation, helping the FBI shut down the deal and track down the bad guys. If they had closed on the deal and been caught, they likely would have faced federal charges as well.

REAL ESTATE FRAUD CRIME STOPPERS ROSTER

Just about everyone identified on the real estate fraud roster is also a potential real estate fraud crime stopper. Homeowners, buyers, sellers, real estate agents, appraisers, loan officers, notaries, and everyone else involved in real estate transactions can play a critical role in shutting down real estate fraud and busting the bad guys. These warriors in the trenches are the first line of defense.

In the following sections, we reveal some additional key players on the real estate and mortgage fraud prevention and protection team.

Record Keepers

Every real estate transaction is a legal transaction, complete with official documentation that must be filed correctly and on a timely basis. Often all you have as a point of reference when closing on a real estate deal are the past records filed on that property. If the records are out of date, everything about the deal becomes suspect.

Protect Yourself

Many professionals remain unlicensed precisely to avoid regulation and prosecution and to fly under the radar. One way to protect yourself from illegal and unethical practices is to insist on working with licensed professionals. For example, you should do the following:

- Make sure the real estate agent you're using is a licensed REALTOR® (a member of the National Association of REALTORS®).

- Work directly with a state-licensed mortgage broker who's a member of the National Association of Mortgage Brokers (NAMB) or obtain your loan directly through the retail loan office of a bank.

- Choose an attorney who's in good standing with the local bar association.

- Use licensed appraisers with an SREA, RM, SRPA, SRA, or MAI designation to verify the market value.

- Hire home inspectors certified through a reputable agency, such as the American Society of Home Inspectors, to confirm the condition of the property.

Who's in charge of keeping the records? Primarily the county clerk, county recorder, or register of deeds, but the title company and closing officers must also be committed to producing accurate and complete records and passing those records to the record keeper on a timely basis.

Regulators

Various agencies regulate real estate professionals on the state and federal level. These agencies define permissible conduct for real estate professionals and discipline their members for failing to follow regulations. Regulators exist for mortgage brokers and loan officers, real estate agents, appraisers, lenders, and attorneys.

Regulators respond to and investigate complaints by consumers, lenders, and other real estate professionals. Although often working with insufficient budgets like other public agencies, they work hard to both define the regulations that govern the professionals and to enforce the rules. Most regulators are able to suspend or revoke the licenses of regulated professionals found to be engaged in fraud and can refer the professionals for criminal investigation and prosecution.

Law Enforcement Agencies and Agents

Federal, state, and local law enforcement agencies often do a fine job of investigating cases of mortgage and real estate fraud and busting the bad guys. However, they're rarely aware of the problem until dozens to hundreds of lenders and homeowners have been conned out of millions of dollars. Sometimes the problem is so rampant and so difficult to discern that it remains undetected for years.

Local, State, and Federal Legislators

Legislators enact laws that criminalize certain conduct as well as laws that require regulation of certain professionals. In May 2005, the State of Georgia enacted the first law in the nation that specifically made mortgage fraud in a residential real estate transaction a crime. Before the Georgia Residential Mortgage Fraud Act became law, state prosecutors were forced to charge those who perpetrated real estate fraud with crimes such as forgery and grand theft. Since the law was enacted, there have been multiple arrests, and numerous other states have moved to adopt similar laws addressing mortgage fraud.

Legislation is key to cracking down on mortgage fraud and other types of real estate fraud, but it's not enough. Laws often are enacted as knee-jerk reactions to articles in newspapers, resulting in vote-producing sound bites and patchwork deterrents. Legislators need to work alongside real estate experts to write laws and implement systemic cures that attack the causes and vulnerabilities in the system, rather than simply prosecuting the perpetrators after fraud has been committed. Chapter 21 explores the challenges and possible solutions in greater depth.

Fraud Busting Begins with You

Although several people sitting around the closing table may be involved in a real estate scam, it takes only one person at that table to stand up and say "No." That person can be you. We encourage you to commit yourself to the S-T-O-P real estate fraud approach:

- **SPOT** fraud by becoming educated about it, which you are doing by reading this book.

- **STOP** fraud by simply refusing to become a part of it. If you become suspicious at closing, you can often take a break, call the lender, and explain why you're suspicious. Lenders are often the primary victim of real estate fraud so the lender is usually the best one to contact. Remember, the mortgage broker is not necessarily the lender! The lender is typically identified on the promissory note, mortgage, deed of trust, and HUD-1 Settlement Statement.

- **POST** scams and schemes you witness to the authorities, so they can investigate, identify the perpetrators, and prosecute them. See the appendix for information on where to report suspected incidents of real estate and mortgage fraud.

4

INFLATED APPRAISALS:

The Root of Many Real Estate Scams

Are you looking to score some quick cash in real estate? If you are, the easiest way to do it is to sell a house for tens or hundreds of thousands of dollars more than it's worth. Another way is to buy a house for more than the seller is asking on the condition that the seller pays you back the surplus. All you have to do is convince an appraiser to claim, in writing, that the property is worth what you say it's worth and then convince an unsuspecting buyer, seller, or lender to believe it. It's not that hard. Con artists do it all the time.

Inflated appraisals are at the root of most real estate scams, including illegal flipping, cash back at closing schemes, and refinancing rip-offs. This chapter examines the key role of the appraiser in protecting everyone's best interests and reveals how a biased appraisal can threaten the fairness of a real estate transaction.

THE APPRAISAL PROCESS

Whenever you purchase a home or borrow money using your home as collateral, your lender sends an appraiser over to the house to estimate its market value. The appraiser inspects the property and uses one of the following three methods to estimate value:

1. *Sales comparison approach.* The appraiser estimates the value of the home based on actual sales prices of similar homes that have recently sold in the same area.
2. *Cost approach.* The appraiser determines how much a similar property would cost to build, or in other words, the cost of replacing the property.
3. *Income approach.* If the property is going to be used as a rental unit, the appraiser checks out the revenue generated by other similar rental properties in the same area.

Ideally, the appraiser is well schooled in appraising properties, follows Uniform Standards of Professional Appraisal Practice (USPAP), and is not swayed by outside influences, such as how much the homeowner wants to borrow, how much the seller wants for the house, or how badly the loan officer wants her client to qualify for a loan. USPAP prohibits appraisers from working toward a target value and requires the appraiser to take specific steps to ensure an accurate appraisal.

An unbiased and accurate appraisal protects the interests of everyone involved in the transaction along with many who are not involved in the transaction:

- The buyers are assured that they're not paying too much for the property.
- The lender knows that the property is worth enough to justify the loan amount.
- Homeowners in the area don't suffer from inflated property values.

Problems Inherent in the Appraisal Industry

Appraisals are intended to be unbiased, but certain factors, such as the following, occasionally influence appraisers, either directly or indirectly:

- Commissioned agents (brokers and loan officers), who originate a large majority of loans, usually order the appraisals. If a loan isn't approved due to a low appraisal, the agent receives no commission. Giving commissioned agents the power to hire the appraiser creates a conflict of interest—the profit motive often drives the agent to select more cooperative, "aggressive" appraisers.
- A loan agent's commission is based on the amount of the loan. The more someone borrows, the more the agent earns, so loan agents may pressure appraisers to come up with higher appraisals.
- Real estate agents are also paid on commission. If a low appraisal prevents a buyer from obtaining financing to purchase a property, the real estate agent doesn't get paid. In addition, the higher the sales price, the more money the agent makes, so few agents, even those who are supposed to be representing the buyer, are motivated to negotiate a lower sales price. Agents often show up during an appraisal to exert personal pressure on the appraiser to come up with the highest possible value.
- Sellers often pressure appraisers to provide an appraisal that supports their asking price or try to influence the appraisal by highlighting certain features of the home and steering them clear of defects. In some cases, buyers even get in on the act, so they can borrow more money and get some cash back at the closing.
- The appraisal process can be somewhat subjective resulting in an appraisal amount that varies depending on the experience and education of the appraiser.
- Appraiser selection is often largely based on price rather than experience and education.

- The work required to develop an accurate appraisal is significant, but the price paid for an appraisal has not increased in many years. To make more money, appraisers have to do more, not better, appraisals.
- Unethical appraisers sometimes choose to make more money by charging extra fees (in the form of bribes or kickbacks) to write up the appraisal for a certain amount. In most cases, however, appraisers who inflate appraisals do it simply to remain in business.

The Lack of Effective Regulation

Ideally, the government or professional organizations would regulate appraisers by monitoring activities, investigating complaints, and imposing some sort of discipline, but that's not happening. There are simply too many complaints, and government agencies don't have the funding necessary to provide effective enforcement. Many states require that appraisers be licensed, but licensing often lowers the bar, requiring appraisals to comply with minimum licensing requirements rather than to obtain certification through professional agencies.

In addition to licensing, states should require appraisers to be certified through a professional organization that requires them to take classes in real estate law and mortgage fraud.

WHY INACCURATE APPRAISALS ARE SO DESTRUCTIVE

When you're in the market for a used car, you can look up the Kelley Blue Book value on the car and get a general idea of how much it's worth. This helps you determine how much to offer for the car. If you're taking out a loan to pay for the car, the Blue Book value gives the lender a good idea of how much the car is worth. It also tells the insurance company how much to insure the car for.

Imagine what would happen if the used car prices in the Kelley Blue Book were influenced by those who were selling the used cars or by buyers who wanted to borrow thousands of dollars more than the car is worth. Used cars would be way overpriced. Lenders would make extremely risky used car loans. Insurance rates on used cars would skyrocket.

Appraisers serve the same function in the housing market as the Kelley Blue Book serves in the used car market. In the following sections, we reveal the negative effects of inflated appraisals.

Making Homes Unaffordable

A single inflated appraisal can ripple through a neighborhood, artificially increasing property values throughout the area. How so? Say one appraiser jacks up the appraised price of a property by a few thousand dollars to meet the price that the buyer and seller agreed on. When another house goes for sale in the same neighborhood, the next appraiser uses the inflated sales price as a comparable value in her appraisal. Homeowners notice that property values are on the rise, and when they place their homes on the market, they increase their asking prices. In a matter of weeks or months, the entire neighborhood is overvalued.

This example assumes that the first appraisal was inflated by just a few thousand dollars. Just imagine what happens in areas where properties are appraised for tens or hundreds of thousands of dollars more than their true market values. An affordable neighborhood suddenly becomes overpriced. First-time buyers may not even be able to purchase into the area because the houses have been priced out of their market.

Inflating Property Taxes

In most parts of the country, property taxes are based on the sales price of the home and reassessments are based on the home prices in the neighborhood. When inflated appraisals result in inflated sales prices, even if these prices are inflated only to cover seller concessions, they result in higher property taxes. And higher property taxes make homes less affordable.

Inflated Appraisal Fallout

We asked Kathy Coon, Chief Appraiser, FNC, to comment on the practice of inflating appraisals and the effect that inflated appraisals have on homeowners and communities. Here's what she had to say:

"I assisted the FBI and U.S. attorney in one of the largest mortgage fraud cases in the country—a case involving Joe Bob Moncrief (Houston, Texas), who was accused of inflating appraisals in a mortgage fraud scheme. In reviewing the appraisals, there was evidence that Moncrief had intentionally inflated the appraised value of numerous houses for the purpose of obtaining mortgage loans. Since appraisals by a licensed or certified appraiser are required for loans for sales or refinances, the participation of an appraiser is necessary for these schemes to take place.

"Moncrief intentionally produced appraisals with values far in excess of the local market. Further, he was paid excessive appraisal fees for providing these appraisals. Although the other participants in the scheme pled prior to trial, Moncrief was tried and convicted. He is currently serving a 23-year term in federal prison.

"Mortgage fraud schemes are taking place throughout the country. Although the typical homeowner is not familiar with these schemes, they are directly affected by the impact of mortgage fraud. First, the local market becomes affected by inflated sales becoming part of the data sources that are used to list, sell, and appraise other homes. After a while, the real estate market corrects itself, but not before numerous houses are sold at inflated prices and cannot be resold or refinanced due to the balance owed. The result is usually foreclosure.

"Another very significant impact to all consumers is the impact of inflated property prices, which are then used by taxing authorities to establish the amount used for taxation. Typically, the prices in mortgage fraud schemes are well beyond the normal market value—sometimes two or three times higher. These amounts, if used by tax districts, result in huge increases in property taxes."

In many areas with inflated property taxes, sellers have to lower the price of their homes so buyers can afford the monthly mortgage payments along with their property tax payments. The initial over-valuation thus results in devaluation driven by tax rates rather than market influences.

Creating a Net Worth Roller Coaster

Over time, real estate naturally appreciates. In areas where inflated appraisals are at work, homes may appreciate 15 to 20 percent or more in a single year, skyrocket over the course of a few years, and then crash. Some homeowners, thinking that their properties will continue to appreciate at over 10 percent annually forever, cash out the equity in their homes by refinancing. When the housing bubble bursts, they find themselves owning a home that's worth less than what they owe on it.

Net worth (the value of what you own minus what you owe) is the best indicator of personal wealth. When net worth is artificially inflated through inflated property values, it often drives homeowners to borrow too much, placing their homes and their future lifestyles at risk.

HOW INACCURATE APPRAISALS CONTRIBUTE TO FRAUD

Inflated appraisals play a key role in most of the real estate and mortgage fraud cases we cover in this book. In the following sections, we reveal the way con artists use inflated (and deflated) appraisals to cash out by misrepresenting the true value of a property.

Cashing Out Nonexistent Equity

When a homeowner needs cash to pay for anything from college tuition to credit card debt to home renovations or a new vehicle, they often cash out the equity in their home by borrowing against it. There's nothing wrong with obtaining a cash-out refinance loan, assuming that equity is really there. In many cases, however, homeowners cash out equity that's not there. The homeowners tell the loan officer how much they need (or want), the loan officer tells the appraiser, and the appraiser writes up an inflated appraisal to secure the loan approval.

The problem with this approach is that the appraisal is no longer related to the true value of the home. It's related to the target that the homeowner and loan officer want the appraiser to hit. Several negative consequences result, such as the following:

- The lender approves a loan based on false information, taking on additional risk that they did not knowingly agree to.
- The homeowners may believe that the appraisal is an accurate indication of the value of the home and decide to invest more money in it for renovations, unaware that additional renovations will not increase the property's value enough to cover the costs of the renovations.
- The homeowners take out a loan that exceeds the value of the property. When the homeowners can't sell the home for enough to pay off the mortgage, they are forced to pay the mortgage shortfall from their savings.
- Property values and taxes in the area increase based on the inflated appraisal.

As a homeowner, you may consider inflated property values to be a good thing because they increase the equity in your home. However, an artificial increase is usually temporary and can lead you into making bad financial decisions. Accurate appraisals enable everyone in the process to make well-informed decisions.

Flipping Scams

Illegal house flipping schemes often involve both deflated and inflated appraisals. A buyer may obtain a deflated appraisal to purchase a property (typically a property that has been foreclosed by a lender) for significantly less than market value. The flipper then performs a little cosmetic work on the house to make it look pretty and obtains an inflated appraisal to sell the property for much more than market value.

In one area in Ohio, a team of illegal house flippers completely controlled property values through inflated appraisals. They eventually succeeded in creating an entire neighborhood of overvalued properties. Then they sold the properties, cashing out the inflated equity and leaving the rest of the residents to deal with the fallout once the housing values leveled out.

Cash Back at Closing Deals

When a buyer receives cash back at the closing, it almost always means that the lender has been duped into approving a loan in excess of the property's market value. The document used to fool the lender is almost always an inflated appraisal.

Predatory Lending

Unethical loan officers, mortgage brokers, and others who "sell" loans are often guilty of predatory lending—convincing homeowners to bite off more than they can chew, financially speaking.

In loan flipping or churning schemes, the loan originator convinces a homeowner to refinance again and again. Obtaining approval for each subsequent loan requires increasingly inflated appraisals. The homeowner is led to believe that the appraisals reflect the true market value of the property and that the property is increasing in value sufficiently to cover the loan amounts. The fact is, however, that the loan officer is stripping the equity from the home through repeat commissions.

Note: The term *flipping* has two meanings, depending on whether it references loans or properties. In relation to mortgage loans, flipping is a predatory lending practice, as discussed above and in chapter 18. Flipping a property (see chapter 7) consists of buying a property and then selling it for significantly more than its true market value.

Builder Bailouts

Builder bailouts often involve the ultimate in phony appraisals. They generally involve completely false appraisals that show a partially constructed or nonexistent property as being completely finished. The lender is led to believe that a home exists when, in fact, it does not.

As chapter 9 reveals, builder bailout schemes become increasingly more common in times of declining home values and sales volumes. Builders begin working on a new subdivision, and when they can't sell homes to cover the costs, they run out of money to complete the project so they manufacture a sale to have the lender bail them out.

Manufactured Housing Scams

Manufactured housing (a mobile home) is sort of a cross between a car and a house. Houses are built off-site and then transported to subdivisions—tracts of land with dirt roads and often no facilities to speak of. These homes are typically appraised at the time of invoice along with the value of the land on which the house will eventually rest, but like a car, as soon as the mobile home is dropped in place, it depreciates significantly.

Inflated appraisals are often used in manufactured housing scams. Used homes may be appraised as if they were brand new. Units may be overvalued. Even the appraisal of the land on which the home sits may be inflated.

Deflated Appraisals

In high-rent districts, where property taxes are in the nose-bleed section, some buyers and sellers are giving themselves a much needed tax break. To cut capital gains taxes and trim property taxes, buyers simply pay a portion of the purchase price in cash, off the books. Buy a million-dollar house for $750,000, slip the seller $250,000 cash under the table, and instead of paying property taxes on a million-dollar property, you pay property taxes on a $750,000 property—and the seller gets to pocket $250,000 in profits, tax free!

Nobody likes to pay skyrocketing property taxes, but scofflaw schemes to lower tax assessments on houses undermine attempts to set home prices accurately and fairly. Ultimately, they increase the tax burden on law-abiding taxpayers.

Accurate appraisals level the playing field and ensure fair pricing, full disclosure, and equitable taxation. Deceptive appraisals, whether inflated or deflated, create situations in which buyers, lenders, and homeowners are misinformed and almost guaranteed to lose out in the long run.

5

LYING FOR DOLLARS I:

Doctoring Loan Applications

A loan application is designed to collect information that enables the lender to assess your overall financial health and your ability to make the monthly payments. Lying on the application fools the lender into approving a risky loan. It's the equivalent of omitting on an application for life insurance that you smoke three packs of cigarettes a day.

Although few people would consider lying on a life insurance application, many people have no qualms about lying on loan applications. Some borrowers believe that because they think they can afford the monthly payments, lying is okay. Others may fudge the numbers so they can achieve their dream of homeownership. Con artists will go so far as to create fictitious borrowers and properties to completely fleece a lender.

This chapter presents the many ways applicants lie on their loan applications and reveals an actual case in which doctored loan applications were used to con lenders out of millions of dollars. We also explain how phone banks and document mills facilitate these scams, and we show you what you can do to protect yourself from becoming a victim or an accomplice.

FUDGING THE FACTS ON LOAN APPLICATIONS

Whenever you apply for a mortgage, you must fill out the 1003 (commonly referred to as the ten-oh-three, or officially as the Uniform Residential Loan Application). Just above the space for your signature is a legal statement worded something like this:

> I/We fully understand that it is a federal crime punishable by fine or imprisonment, or both, to knowingly make any false statements concerning any of the above facts as applicable under the provisions of Title 18, United States Code, Section 1001, et seq.

Few people read this statement, understand it, or pay attention to it. They complete the form with the help of their loan officer, or the loan officer completes the form for them. Then they simply sign the form, assuming that the loan officer or whoever's advising them has entered the correct information.

In the following sections, we highlight areas of the 1003 where people commonly provide false information. By knowing the most vulnerable areas, you're better equipped to spot false information on a 1003, whether it's your application or someone else's.

Faking Employment and Income

Parts IV and V of the 1003 request employment and income information. The borrowers' monthly income provides a fairly good indication of the monthly mortgage payment they can afford and is the information that the lender uses to determine whether borrowers qualify for a particular loan.

Applicants, loan officers, and con artists can jot down any employment information and monthly income they can imagine, but then most loan programs require them to provide some sort of verification. This is where the scheme gets a little complicated, but verifying employment is still fairly easy, as you can note in the following steps:

1. A borrower gets a friend or relative who owns a business to say that the borrower works there.
2. The borrower or loan officer can use a program such as Quick-Books to generate the pay stubs and W-2 forms required to build a solid employment history. (Of course, lenders try to validate these documents and the information they contain by calling the business, reverse-checking telephone numbers, and performing employer I.D. searches.)
3. Internet sites provide an assortment of services to verify employment, including phony pay stubs, employment verification letters, and phone verifications. The borrower simply signs a contract as employee and pays a fee, and the company verifies that the borrower works there.

More complex schemes may involve phone banks with telephone lines that are registered to nonexistent employers. When a lender calls to verify employment, someone answers the phone in the name of the nonexistent business and verifies that the borrower works there.

Stealing Identities

Identity theft is the fastest growing white-collar crime and is used in a variety of ways to cheat people out of money. In real estate and mortgage fraud, con artists use stolen identities to purchase properties and apply for loans. In Georgia, a closing attorney spearheaded a house flipping scheme that involved the theft of college students' identities for use on loan applications. The attorney's crime ring was found guilty of illegally flipping more than 100 properties and scamming lenders out of more than $20 million.

Stolen identities are often used to purchase properties out of state because the victim usually must file a police report in the state where the property is located. That's right—the *victim* must travel to another state to seek justice. A con artist can often use a single identity to secure several loans because the loan typically takes three months to show up on the person's credit report, and most people rarely check their credit reports.

Sharing Credit Histories

A credit score of 700 or higher helps borrowers qualify for the largest loans at the lowest interest rates. You can boost your credit score legitimately by borrowing money and paying your bills on time. Some shady Internet companies have found a faster, easier way to boost your credit score—you simply add your name to a credit card account of someone who has a high credit limit and solid history.

Say you have a credit card with a high credit limit. You use the card often and do a pretty good job of paying down the balance. You can add your son or daughter or another family member to your card, and it instantly improves the family member's credit score. This is somewhat of a gray area in our estimation, but it's not illegal.

Credit-sharing companies have taken the practice one step further. They recruit people who have high credit scores and then pay them to add people with lousy credit to their accounts. Someone with bad credit pays the company a few hundred or thousands of dollars, the company adds the person's name to the accounts of several people who have good credit histories, and voila, the person's credit score immediately jumps into the desired range. When the credit score is used to fool a lender into approving a risky loan, it is fraud, pure and simple.

Renting Assets

Part VI of the 1003 requests a complete record of assets (what you own) and liabilities (what you owe). Using this information, the lender can determine your net worth, another factor the lender uses to determine your creditworthiness.

For people who don't own much stuff but have a lot of debt, Part VI of the 1003 can raise some lender red flags. To help, some companies on the Internet offer asset rental services. For a fee, these companies can show you as owning any of the following assets:

- Savings account with plenty of money in it
- Checking account with an impressive balance
- CD (certificate of deposit)
- Cars, boats, yachts, airplanes—you name it

In many cases, all the lender can do is call and check on the existence and value of the asset. With a savings account or CD, the lender may ask how long the money has been available. Because the accounts were in existence before you were added as an account holder, the funds are verified as *seasoned*, that is, it appears as though you've owned the asset for quite a while.

Financial institutions won't generally verify whether other people are also listed as account holders because it might violate confidentiality obligations to those other people. So the lender can't really confirm that the account does not have multiple account holders. In other words, they may add hundreds of people's names to an account and make it look as though you're the sole account holder.

Here's an excerpt from an actual email message sent out to real estate professionals to help them close on deals in which borrowers would have trouble verifying their assets or employment:

From: Linda Goering
Sent: Wednesday, August 03, 2005, 2:37 P.M.
To: (name omitted)
Subject: Asset Rental—Verification of Employment

Hi, Joe.

It was nice speaking with you today. Hopefully, this email will provide solutions to you like it has to so many other mortgage brokers and financial advisors over the years. The following is a brief explanation of our programs. Several files are also attached to this email.

ASSET RENTAL PROGRAM

The Asset Rental Program is a terrific tool which enables you to "save" clients you would otherwise lose due to their inability to show sufficient assets. Seasoning is available.

The 5% fee is usually recovered thru your normal closing fees or your client can simply pay the fee directly up front.

- Asset Rental Program Files Attached
- Asset Rental Brochure
- Asset Rental Application

EMPLOYMENT VERIFICATION PROGRAM

The Employment Verification Program is a popular service which can help you "save" clients who can't verify the required employment data.

Employment Verification Program Files Attached

- Form A (Independent Contractor Agreement)
- Form B (VOE Request)

If you have any questions, feel free to contact me. I look forward to talking with you again soon.

Linda Goering
VP Marketing

Fortunately, soon after they were notified of this operation, federal authorities shut down the site. Yet as soon as they shut down this operation, two more opened up. Cracking down on these and other Internet-based fraud facilitators is nearly impossible.

No-Down-Payment Loans

Lenders typically require a 20 percent down payment on a home loan because history shows that homeowners who have 20 percent invested in a home are less likely to default on their loans. Lenders may accept a much lower percentage down payment from borrowers who agree to take out private mortgage insurance (PMI). Some lenders also allow buyers to participate in home loan assistance programs.

Some companies and individuals have developed novel ways to finance the down payment without letting the lender know about it, including the following:

- *Silent second.* The buyer takes out a separate (second) mortgage to cover the down payment and closing costs without revealing the loan to the lender who's approving the first mortgage.
- *Commission program.* The buyer enrolls the seller in a "program." The seller pays a fee plus an amount equivalent to the down payment into the program. As a commission for enrolling the seller, the buyer receives the amount needed to cover the down payment. An inflated appraisal convinces the lender to approve a loan that covers the seller's fee and down payment.
- *Prepurchase home equity loans.* Through some creative financing, the buyers take out a home equity loan on the property they're about to purchase. The company deposits the amount into an escrow account, showing that the buyers have enough to cover the down payment. The buyers then pay back the down payment through the escrow account.
- *Inflated purchase prices.* The buyer and seller agree to a purchase price and then enter into a purchase contract showing a purchase price that is 20 percent higher than the actual purchase price. Either the buyer doesn't deposit any down payment toward the closing and the closing agent prepares the paperwork reflecting that the borrower brought the 20 percent down payment, or the seller deposits the 20 percent down payment and receives it back from the sales proceeds.

These no-down-payment programs result in several misrepresentations:

- The buyers aren't actually making the required down payment, but on paper, it looks as though they are, which makes them appear more financially well off than they really are.
- The buyers are essentially taking out a loan to cover the down payment and not disclosing this loan (liability) on the 1003.
- The sales price is usually inflated to kick back money to the seller or buyer to cover the down payment and any fees associated with the scheme.

CASE STUDY

Following is an actual case of mortgage fraud reported by the United States Department of Justice. We edited the actual press release for length:

Snellville Lawyer Pleads Guilty
in Mortgage Fraud Scheme

September 26, 2006. According to United States Attorney David E. Nahmias, Michael Hipe (a Snellville, Georgia lawyer) and codefendant Eric Friedman became partners in a used car dealership in Atlanta called Hipe Motors. In order to raise money for the business, Hipe purchased four new condominiums. Eric Friedman prepared false loan applications and supporting documentation, including tax returns that misrepresented Hipe's income. At the real estate closings, Hipe signed the false loan applications, certifying them as accurate.

To pull money out from the closings, Friedman and Hipe misrepresented to lenders that a portion of the loan proceeds would be used for the renovation and construction of the condominiums, though no renovations were needed. They

Spotting the **S**igns

Misleading information on loan applications and other strategies designed to deceive lenders are all a part of mortgage fraud. Most of the warning signs are readily evident on the 1003 that the borrower fills out when applying for the loan and is required to sign at closing. Beware of the following:

- A loan officer, real estate agent, or someone else involved in the transaction encourages you to claim that you have a higher income or a second job that you don't actually have.

- You've never been asked to complete or review a loan application or someone tells you not to worry about it—they'll take care of everything.

- You're encouraged to claim that you have more assets than you really have.

- A company offers to pay you so they can list someone on your credit card account or another account.

- An Internet site claims to be able to increase your credit score by allowing you to "piggyback" on other people's accounts.

- A company offers to verify nonexistent employment or income for you.

- A loan officer or someone else completes your loan application for you and asks that you sign it without reviewing it, or the person asks that you sign an incomplete loan application (which they can fill out with any information they want later).

- A loan application has entries that have been whited out and "corrected."

- You don't have sufficient funds to make the required down payment and someone presents a clever plan that allows you to purchase the property without a down payment—a plan that requires you to lie about the purchase price or the existence or source of the down payment.

- You're taking out a loan to cover the down payment, and that loan is not listed on the loan application for the first mortgage.

claimed that the construction work was to be performed by "The Fabricators, Inc.," a shell company not incorporated in the State of Georgia. Friedman and Hipe used the money to finance Hipe Motors and for Eric Friedman's personal expenses. The funds obtained at closings were run through Hipe's bank accounts and then run through Eric and Brianne Friedman's bank accounts.

When Hipe was unable to obtain further financing to purchase condominiums, he introduced his mother and a family friend, both of whom live and work in Massachusetts, to Friedman. Friedman persuaded Hipe's mother to act as a straw buyer on the purchase of three condominiums in Atlanta to provide additional funds to operate Hipe Motors. He prepared loan applications containing false information and supporting documentation, including tax returns that misrepresented Hipe's mother's employment and income. At two of the three real estate closings for his mother, Hipe and Friedman acted as her attorneys, executing numerous documents, including the loan applications.

Eric Friedman also persuaded Hipe's family friend to provide him with his credit information. Once Friedman obtained that information, he opened a checking account at Wachovia Bank in the name of the family friend. In June 2002, at Friedman's behest, the family friend purchased a home in Braselton, Georgia, for the sole purpose of pulling money out of the transaction to further finance Hipe Motors. That transaction was also financed through the submission of a false loan application prepared by Eric Friedman. Then, in February of 2004, the family friend sold the Braselton property to another straw purchaser/borrower (Timothy Bauer) to obtain even more money for the scam.

As a result of the scam, lenders foreclosed on all seven of Hipe's condominiums (with losses exceeding $500,000).

For his part, Hipe pleaded guilty to one count of conspiracy to commit mail fraud. He could receive a maximum sentence of five years in prison and a fine of up to $250,000. Sentencing for Hipe has not been scheduled.

Protect Yourself

Whenever you sign a loan application, you're representing, at the risk of committing a felony, that the information on that loan application is accurate and true. To avoid becoming a victim or accomplice of mortgage fraud, take the following steps:

- Never sign a loan application that is incomplete—someone can fill in the blanks with false information later.
- Read every copy of the loan application and correct any inaccuracies before you sign it. The application is usually presented prior to closing and again as part of the closing package; review it prior to closing and check it again at closing.
- Don't follow the advice of someone who encourages you to overestimate your income or assets.
- Don't get conned by websites or companies offering to provide you with false documents, including novelty paycheck stubs, falsified tax returns, or asset rentals.
- Work with licensed and reputable real estate professionals who are affiliated with professional organizations.
- If you see any suspicious activity before or during the closing, stop the transaction, contact the lender immediately, and report the incident to authorities. (Refer to the appendix for details on how to report suspected fraud in your state.)

On August 23, 2006, Eric Friedman pleaded guilty to conspiracy to commit mail fraud, attempt to evade the payment of income taxes, credit card fraud, and interstate transportation of cars obtained by fraud. He could receive a maximum sentence of 40 years in prison and a fine of up to $1,250,000. No sentencing date has been scheduled for Friedman.

6

CASH BACK AT CLOSING SCHEMES

Cash back deals are stitched into the very fabric of the U.S. economy. Manufacturers promote their products with cash rebates. Credit card companies offer cash back on purchases. Even banks dangle cash back deals to attract new customers. Now homebuyers and con artists are jumping on the cash back bandwagon, and plenty of real estate professionals—people who should know better—are tripping over themselves to cater to them.

In this chapter, we expose cash back at closing arrangements for what they really are—mortgage fraud. We explain why they're so tempting, how these deals unfold, and what you can do to avoid getting involved in these schemes.

WHAT IS CASH BACK AT CLOSING?

On its surface, cash back at closing seems like a win-win situation. The buyer simply pays a little more for a property than it's worth, and the seller agrees to kick back the surplus cash to the buyer. For buyers, it can be a savvy financial move, allowing them to pay off outstanding credit card debt or use the extra cash for home repairs, renovations, or that vacation they always wanted. The seller unloads his house at close to or better than his asking price. The real estate agent gets a bigger commission. The loan officer chalks up another successful loan. And the lender scores a larger loan and stands to earn more interest over the life of the loan.

Unfortunately, as with most deals that seem too good to be true, cash back at closing schemes are just another way of scamming someone—in this case, the lender, who's fooled into making an under-collateralized loan. But lenders aren't the only losers. Buyers often end up with loans that they can't afford. Housing values in the area are artificially inflated, making housing less affordable and raising property taxes. Honest real estate agents lose business to dishonest agents who offer cash back deals. And neighborhoods begin to buckle when homeowners default on the inflated loans and their properties end up in foreclosure.

Artificially Inflating the Appraisal

The excess cash available at closing almost always results from an inflated appraisal, as we discussed in chapter 4. In areas where property values are declining, cash back at closing deals become more prevalent. Unable to find buyers, sellers will do almost anything to unload their house, especially if they can obtain their asking price. A home may linger on the market for months at a much lower price and then suddenly a buyer purchases the property, agreeing to pay significantly more than the asking price. At closing, the seller simply kicks the extra money back to the buyer or to whomever set up the deal.

Convincing the Buyer That It's Okay

Buyers are often easy marks for cash back at closing schemes because, quite frankly, who couldn't use a little extra money? Buyers may need extra cash to cover the down payment or closing costs,

---

Whatever the **M**oney's **U**sed **F**or, **I**t's **W**rong

---

People often justify cash back at closing arrangements by focusing on the good deeds they plan to accomplish with the extra cash. Some use the extra money to finance the down payment and closing costs. Others roll the money right back into the property, using it for repairs and renovations intended to increase the property's value. Some people buy cars or furniture, pay for vacations, catch up on their credit card payments, cover medical expenses, or simply pocket the cash. Fooling a lender into approving a loan based on false information is wrong, no matter how you spend the money.

---

unpaid bills, or college expenses, or they may simply want to use the extra money to renovate the property. Late-night TV real estate gurus promote cash back at closing, and most people don't even realize that anything is wrong with it.

In some cases, the buyer doesn't even receive the extra cash because the excess money is paid to a company controlled by the loan officer or real estate broker. In others, the money is funneled out as finder's fees, assignment fees, or commissions.

Convincing the Seller That It's Okay

Sellers usually want one thing—to have someone purchase their home quickly at or near their asking price—and, in a declining market, they're willing to go along with just about anything that will make that happen. When a seller becomes a little suspicious and hesitant about moving forward on a cash back at closing deal, whoever is pushing the deal may try to convince the seller that the deal is above board for the following reasons:

- The seller will get the full sales price.
- The buyer will use the extra money to renovate the property.
- The lender is fully aware of what's going on.

- The funds will be paid directly to a contractor for work on the property.
- The extra funds will be used to pay off a second lien that the buyer has placed against the property. (This second lien may be for a second mortgage used to make the down payment and pay closing costs.)

CASE STUDY

A surprising number of real estate professionals believe that cash back at closing arrangements are perfectly legal. Real estate agents, mortgage specialists, and others who should know better frequently approach us and describe cash back deals that they were convinced were legitimate.

Recently, a top-selling real estate agent in Florida listed a house for $600,000. A broker who wasn't from the area had a buyer interested in purchasing the property. Although the broker and buyer had never seen the property, they submitted an offer of $695,000—$95,000 more than the asking price! The only hitch was that the buyer wanted the seller to kick back the extra $95,000 to the buyer at closing. The seller just wanted to sell the house, so he had no problem with the offer. The seller's agent was concerned, but the seller's attorney had informed the seller that nothing was wrong with such a transaction. Unfortunately, the seller's attorney was ill-informed.

The law that governs these transactions is referenced on the 1003, Uniform Residential Loan Application, that every buyer signs when she applies for a loan—Title 18, United States Code, Section 1001. It's part of the small print that lawyers always tell you to read closely before signing anything. To paraphrase Title 18, section 1001, you can't lie on a loan application or any other document related to the transaction. When a buyer, seller, appraiser, real estate agent, loan officer, or another party provides a false statement of the property's value, misrepresents the sales price on the purchase contract submitted to the lender, or misrepresents the sales price or the

Spotting the Signs

Cash back at closing arrangements generally involve mortgage fraud. Whenever any information about the transaction is not disclosed in the loan documents, the lender has been misled and the deal is fraudulent. Learn to spot the following signs of cash back at closing deals:

- As a seller, you're asked to sign a purchase agreement offering an amount that's significantly higher than your asking price.

- The appraisal is obviously inflated—the house is valued at thousands or even hundreds of thousands more than comparable properties in the same area.

- As a buyer, your real estate agent or loan officer tells you that you can qualify for a higher loan amount and suggests that you obtain the higher loan and take the excess cash back at closing.

- A house lingers on the market with a low asking price and then suddenly sells for or relists at an amount much higher than the asking price.

- Neither the buyer nor the buyer's agent has ever seen the property, but they're willing to offer significantly more than the list price.

- When the listing agent (seller's agent) picks the title company and the buyer wants to use a different title company than the seller or seller's agent has chosen.

- You can't afford the down payment on a house, but the loan officer tells you that you can simply agree to pay more for the house to cover the down payment and closing costs.

- The buyer or buyer's agent claims that the extra money will be used for home repairs or renovations or paid to a contracting company to handle the repairs or renovations.

actual disposition of proceeds on the HUD-1 Settlement Statement, they're lying. Engaging in these misrepresentations can also violate the federal mail fraud, wire fraud, and bank fraud statutes—depending on how the documents are submitted and the type of entity that funds or purchases the loan. One rationalization often used is that the agreement to pay cash to the buyer is a "side deal" or a "separate contract," and therefore the parties are not making any type of misrepresentation—after all, people can agree to anything "after" the loan is funded, right? Unfortunately, this is not correct. Because the agreement actually existed prior to the time the loan was obtained, it isn't a "separate contract" or a "side deal." It is a material contract term. By applying for a mortgage loan and hiding one of these deals, the participants are committing mortgage fraud.

CASE STUDY

In some cases, con artists combine two or more schemes to invent a new way to fleece homeowners and investors. Attorney John Jacobs describes a scheme in which con artists employed cash back at closing and illegal flipping to target unsophisticated real estate investors:

"Various companies advertise "free" real estate investment seminars on the Web. Such sites typically encourage visitors to attend a seminar to learn how to profit by buying, renting, and selling homes. To attend the seminar, registrants must provide their name, address, and Social Security number, which the company uses to pull the person's credit report. Prior to the seminar, the company has already targeted the people with the best FICO credit scores—people who are most likely to qualify for large loans. At some point during the seminar, the instructor or another person from the company approaches a well-qualified attendee and pitches a 'great investment opportunity.'

"We encountered an attempted fraud, which to our knowledge did not occur, involving a home that had been listed for over a year at $1.5 million. The company offering the investment seminar offered to pay the asking price if the seller would relist the home for $3 million. The company told the would-be investor that they had found a $3 million home for sale that the investor could purchase for $2.2 million plus $200,000 for renovations (a total investment

Protect Yourself

Whenever the lender is not informed, in writing, of the true nature of the transaction, the transaction is fraudulent. If you go along with the scheme, you become an accomplice, subject to prosecution. Take the following actions to protect yourself and others:

- As a seller, never agree to sign a purchase agreement that reflects the purchase price as higher than what you previously agreed to accept for the property.
- As a seller, don't increase the price of the property to cover concessions you made to the buyer. The price of the property and the concessions you agree to must remain separate; otherwise, they're not really concessions and you're misleading the lender as to the value of the property or the purchase price.
- As a buyer, if you need funds to renovate the property, close on the first mortgage and then apply for a second mortgage or home equity loan to finance the renovations. Lenders often require the funds for renovations to be escrowed so they can monitor the work and make sure it's done.
- If you're being told that you can receive cash back at closing, be very skeptical and try to talk directly to the lender. Make sure that the HUD-1 Settlement Statement correctly reflects the transaction. The HUD-1 should show no increased purchase price and must specify the amount of money being paid out and the identity of the person who's receiving the payout.

New labels have recently emerged to describe cash back at closing schemes. The current labels of choice are "cash back after closing," "unforeseen equity," and "cash reserve." As real estate educator Marge Fraser explains, however, "If you put a raincoat on a duck, it's still a duck." Regardless of what those who are pushing the scheme choose to call it, if the buyer is getting cash back at closing, the transaction very likely involves some type of mortgage fraud.

of $2.4 million). The investor would take out a mortgage of $2.4 million, which would be paid to the company. The company would pay $1.5 million to the seller, $200,000 to the buyer, and walk away with a net profit of about $700,000. Unfortunately, the buyer would owe $2.4 million on a house worth less than $1.5 million."

So, what should you do when faced with one of these schemes? Put a stop to it! Inform all parties that cash back at closing schemes are fraudulent and refuse to participate. You can also call the lender to inform them of the scheme. The lender's phone number is on the closing papers, and they're usually very eager to hear when someone's trying to pull the wool over their eyes.

7

FLIPPING A PROPERTY TO ARTIFICIALLY INFLATE ITS VALUE

Is that house you're about to buy really worth what the appraiser claims it's worth? You might assume that an appraisal is legitimate, but inflated appraisals are often at the root of flipping scams. The appraiser artificially jacks up the property value so a coconspirator can qualify for a bloated loan, cash out the equity, and leave an overpriced, vacant home in his wake or unload the property on an unsuspecting buyer.

In this chapter, we differentiate between legitimate real estate investors who flip houses for profit from those who employ flipping as part of a scam to fleece lenders and homeowners. We show you how to protect yourself from becoming a victim or unwitting accomplice in an illegal house flipping scheme, and we feature a case study to illustrate just how bold some of these illegal flippers really are.

FLIPPING HOUSES FOR PROFIT: THE RIGHT WAY AND THE WRONG WAY

In the real estate industry and in legal circles, "flip" is a four-letter word. In FR (Final Rule)-4615 Prohibition of Property Flipping, HUD has refused to insure loans for certain flipped properties. Why? Because illegal flipping artificially inflates housing values, increases the incidence of loan defaults, and commonly results in a rash of vacant properties and foreclosures.

To consumers who read books on flipping houses as a way of investing in real estate and watch shows like *Flip This House* and *Flip That House,* however, flipping is a perfectly legitimate way to profit in real estate. As you see in the following sections, both schools of thought are correct.

Flipping Legitimately, as an Investor

Flipping houses as an investor is a legitimate strategy for making money in real estate. You buy a property below market value, fix it up (or not), and sell it for a price that's in line with current market values.

Investors who flip houses the right way can earn a reasonable profit by buying, renovating, and selling properties. This fix-it-and-flip-it approach has a positive effect on the real estate market. It increases property values, improves neighborhoods, and provides quality housing for those who need it. It contributes to the American dream of homeownership. It's capitalism at its best.

Flipping the Wrong Way, as a Con Artist

The dark side of house flipping consists of criminals artificially inflating property values and selling overpriced homes to ill-informed buyers or cashing out the inflated equity, sticking the lender with the bill, and leaving a legacy of foreclosures and vacancies. Because of this, many lenders refuse to approve loans for flipping properties or they apply strict conditions to these sales.

Illegal flipping destroys credit ratings, raises interest rates, and ruins neighborhoods. Over the long haul, it threatens the American dream of homeownership. It is unethical, immoral, and illegal.

Illegal flipping typically requires an entire team of coconspirators, including the following:

- *Ringleader.* The ringleader drafts people for the flipping team, convincing the loan officer, appraiser, buyer, and seller to go along with the deal or simply fooling everyone into thinking that the transaction is legitimate.
- *Buyer.* The person buying the home is either the victim or is in on the deal, agreeing to pay more for the home than it's worth. Why would anyone pay significantly more for a property than what it's worth? Usually, an unsuspecting buyer simply gets duped by a con artist or is being paid to lend her credit to the transaction (i.e., the purchaser is acting as a *straw buyer*). Sometimes, however, the buyer knowingly agrees to pay more because she has no intention of paying back the inflated mortgage.
- *Seller.* The homeowner selling the property may or may not be involved in the scam. In some cases, the homeowner simply sells the property to the recruiter at market value, which is not a crime. In other cases, however, the homeowner is a key player in the scam, agreeing to sell the property at a price significantly higher than its market value and kicking back some money to the buyer or the ringleader.
- *Loan officer.* The loan officer simply submits and obtains approval for a loan in excess of the property's market value. In some cases, they're unaware of the property's real value. In many cases, however, the loan officer conspires with the appraiser to jack up the appraisal or simply does not perform his due diligence in obtaining an unbiased appraisal.

Spotting the Signs of Illegal Flipping

When you read a description of illegal flipping, the operation seems transparently obvious, but flippers employ some savvy strategies to fool you into thinking that what they're doing is okay. When buying or selling a property, look for the following signs of an illegal flipping operation:

- The buyer seeks to have the purchase contract written for an amount significantly higher than the asking price.

- The buyer insists that the sales contract indicate the buyer can be an "assignee."

- An appraiser agrees to appraise the home without looking at it or by simply driving past the property rather than going inside.

- An appraiser offers to write up an appraisal in line with your asking price (if you're a seller) or in line with the amount of money you want to borrow (if you're a buyer). In some cases, the appraiser may even ask for an additional fee for this service.

- The appraisal is based on comparable properties located in pricier neighborhoods or properties that are in no way similar to the property you're selling or buying.

- The price of the house you're selling or buying is much higher than the recent sales prices of similar homes in the area.

- The seller is not the owner of record on the property.

- *Appraiser.* The key player in an illegal flipping operation is the appraiser, who inflates the value of the house on paper to enable the buyer to qualify for a higher loan. Sometimes, a real appraiser is pulled into the scheme. In other cases, the appraisal is simply a phony document.

Con artists have devised a host of strategies for profiting from illegal flipping. In the simplest case, the con artist buys a property, enlists the aid of an appraiser to inflate the appraisal, and then sells the overpriced home to an unsuspecting buyer—often someone who can't qualify for a conventional loan. The con artist approaches the desperate buyer and offers to help secure financing to purchase the home and perhaps provide the buyer with a little cash back in the process. The buyer typically ends up owing much more on the house than what it's worth, and often much more than they can afford, and they eventually default on the loan and end up in foreclosure.

In more complicated house flipping schemes, several buyers and sellers work together to sell the house to one another, inflating the value with each transaction. Then, they either cash out the equity one final time and leave the property vacant or sell it to a buyer who gets stuck with a grossly overpriced piece of property.

CASE STUDY

In the Twin Cities of Minneapolis and St. Paul, Minnesota, a house flipper working in cahoots with a crooked appraiser scammed 200 homeowners before being caught.

The flipper acted as the ringleader. He would find a low-priced, often dilapidated home at a price of about $50,000 in an area close to a neighborhood with significantly higher property values. He then recruited an appraiser to write up an inflated appraisal stating that the home's value was somewhere in the range of $100,000.

After taking possession of the property, the ringleader started shopping for buyers in churches and homeless shelters—people who wanted to buy a home but couldn't qualify for a loan. The ringleader offered to help the buyers secure a loan for $70,000 and then take out a second mortgage to cover the remaining $30,000.

When the ringleader found willing buyers, he helped them submit a loan application to a subprime lender in another state thousands of miles away, where the lender had no idea of the property's true market value. The loan would often be a bad loan for the buyers—an adjustable-rate mortgage with a high cap—meaning the interest rate would almost certainly skyrocket shortly after the buyers took possession of the home. The ringleader paid all the closing costs, so the homeowners would get some cash back at closing to cover repairs and renovations or to go shopping.

P*rotect* Y*ourself*

To avoid purchasing a property for more than what it's worth or becoming an unwitting accomplice in a house flipping scam, take the following precautions:

- Check recent sales prices of comparable homes in the same area to ensure that the appraisal is at least relatively accurate.

- Obtain your own appraisal from an appraiser that you hire directly. Accompany the appraiser on the inspection and make sure your appraiser does not have independent contact with the seller, loan officer, real estate agent, or other parties.

- Obtain a home inspection. In illegal flips, cosmetic repairs are often performed to make the home look as though it has been renovated.

- Check the title to make sure the person who is selling you the house is the legal owner. In some cases, flippers will sell a house when the real owners are on vacation.

- If you suspect a problem, consult your own real estate agent, loan officer, or bank, no matter how much someone else tries to convince you not to—and *especially* if someone tries to convince you not to.

The ringleader then helped the homeowners apply for a second mortgage for the remaining $30,000, which placed a second lien on the property. In several cases, the ringleader applied for the loan unbeknownst to the homeowners, using the previous loan application to secure the loan. In other cases, the ringleader simply lied to the homeowners, claiming they wouldn't have to pay off the second mortgage until they sold the house.

The homeowners now owned a $50,000 house with a $100,000 mortgage they probably wouldn't be able to pay, and the con artist walked away with a little less than $50,000 in cash.

8

THE DOUBLE-SALES SCAM:

Selling the Same House Twice

Imagine paying hundreds of thousands of dollars for a home and then arriving to move in only to find another family living there who claims to have bought the home from the same owner. This is exactly what happens in the double-sales scam. The fraudster sells the same property two or more times to different buyers, often over the course of several days or weeks, pockets the proceeds, and leaves the new owners to sort out the mess. In some cases, the person selling the house isn't even the legal owner!

This chapter introduces the double-sales scam and presents an actual case study in which a con artist sold a house three times. What happened? How was it resolved? What could have been done to prevent it? The answers are all in this chapter.

WHAT IS THE DOUBLE-SALES SCAM?

The double-sales scam is one of the oldest cons in the world. Some fraudsters have used it to sell burial plots. The con artist would acquire a burial plot and then sell it to dozens of different people. Sometimes, he wouldn't even buy the plot—he would simply draw up documentation for an existing plot where someone was already buried. Each person who bought the plot would receive a certificate showing that they owned it. None of the buyers would ever realize that they'd been conned. Only when they passed away and their families discovered that someone was already buried there would the scam be revealed. By that time, the con artist was usually long gone.

In some areas, particularly areas where real estate transactions are recorded several weeks to several months after closing, the double-sales scam is commonly used to rip off homebuyers. The con artist lists the home, sells it, and before the buyer can move into the home, the con artist sells it again. Some practitioners of the double-sales scam can sell a home three or four times in a matter of weeks before the first transaction is recorded. Subsequent buyers have no way of knowing that the first transaction took place because when they closed on their transactions, no record of that first transaction was available.

Buying a House—Or Not

To sell a house, you must have a house to sell. To practitioners of the double-sales scam, this is a minor obstacle. Con artists have devised all sorts of clever schemes for acquiring a property to sell, including the following:

- Buying a home
- Taking possession of a vacant home
- Breaking into a home when the homeowners take an extended vacation or have a lengthy stay in a hospital
- Renting a home and drawing up some phony documents proving ownership

Rarely do double-sales scammers buy the property. To make themselves look like the legal owners of the property, they simply record a forged deed showing the transfer of title from the legal owners to them. If a mortgage is recorded against the property, the con artists also file a false satisfaction of mortgage or, in a deed of trust state, they file a forged *reconveyance* of the trust deed—a phony document that shows the mortgage has been paid in full. Falsifying these documents is easy—all that's needed is a notary stamp proving the validity of all the falsified signatures.

Selling to Two or More Buyers

Acquiring a property to use in the scam is pretty straightforward. Selling the property two or more times to different buyers is more of a challenge, but the fraudsters have devised several ways to pull it off:

- They place the house on the market and sell it, just like most homeowners sell their homes. Often, these properties are offered for sale at deep discounts in order to obtain multiple offers.
- They market the property privately as a great investment. In such cases, recruiters typically attend real estate investment seminars or infiltrate investor groups and pitch the property to eager investors who have the cash or financing to quickly purchase the property.
- They process the buyers' loans through different lenders to avoid detection. Currently, lenders have no central database to determine if two or more loans are being applied for to purchase the same property.
- They schedule closings close together at different title companies or involve a title company in the scam.
- They focus on an area with long delays between the closing and when the transaction is officially recorded.

Sometimes, the seller doesn't plan the double sale in advance. The person purchases the property with no intent of selling it to two buyers. A few weeks or months later, when she's in the process of selling the property, she notices that the person from whom she purchased the property is still listed on the title as the owner. The seller seizes the opportunity to sell the property again to another buyer. This scenario isn't all that common—it generally occurs only with vacant property or in unusual situations.

WHO SUFFERS?

As we discuss in chapter 2, real estate and mortgage fraud harm just about everyone. In double-sales scams, the title underwriters that provide the title insurance usually suffer the most. Who foots the bill depends on the state, but generally, it breaks down like this:

1. The buyer who first purchases the property and records the deed takes title to the property, assuming the con artist actually owned the property.
2. Title insurance protects all subsequent buyers whose deeds are later recorded.
3. Title insurance also protects the first buyer if the con artist sold a property she didn't actually own.

Although double-sales scams inconvenience buyers, the buyers generally don't lose money. If the title company is involved in the scam, however, or an escrow company is involved and doesn't actually pay the title insurer for the title policy, the buyer may lose both the home and the money.

CASE STUDY

A seasoned investor from California had bought and renovated several houses in the Detroit area and successfully leased them out. Word of his success and his need for more properties quickly spread through the area so sellers and sellers' agents began calling him.

Spotting the Signs

With all the paperwork you have to fill out at a closing and all the real estate professionals sitting around the closing table, you might think that a double-sales scam would be impossible to execute. Without timely recordings of transactions, however, the scam is fairly easy. To protect yourself, remain on the lookout for the following warning signs:

- The mortgage on the property being sold was recently paid off. Sellers typically pay off the mortgage with proceeds from the sale. They don't generally pay off mortgages right before they sell.

- The person who's selling the property took title recently without recording a mortgage at the same time. Buyers rarely pay cash for properties. They typically take out a loan so the property should have both a deed and mortgage with the seller's name.

- Someone's offering you a great deal on an investment property that's not listed for sale through a broker or public listing, such as the MLS (multiple listing service).

- The recording and signing dates on the documents draw suspicion. If you see that a deed or mortgage was signed in 2002 and not recorded until 2006, something's obviously wrong. The documents may have been forged and the signing dates manipulated to try to show that the person selling the house has owned it for several years. The signing date is easily manipulated, so focus on the recording date.

One such agent was representing a young man who had lost his father and inherited the father's home. The investor purchased the property from the young man.

A few months later, the investor was contacted by another party who claimed to have purchased the same property. The buyers said that the young man had sold the house to them, and they had a signed purchase agreement to prove that they had purchased the house prior to the date on which the investor purchased it. They had not closed on the sale, however, so the investor was the legal owner.

In that case, the investor had no way of knowing that a prior purchase agreement had been signed. He had not acted improperly. The seller was at fault.

Protect Yourself

Getting stuck with making monthly payments on a house you don't own can be devastating. To prevent this from happening to you, take the following precautions prior to closing:

- Analyze the preliminary title report or title commitment for unusual transactions. Your title company can supply you with a title commitment prior to closing.

- Ask the title company that's handling the closing for a 24-month property history, including a history of all mortgages. Look for mortgages that recently have been paid in full, which is out of the ordinary.

- Purchase title insurance, and make sure it's paid for at or prior to closing rather than having the policy paid out of escrow. In double-sales scams, good title insurance may be your only safety net.

- Obtain a closing protection letter from the title company. This provides you with some additional legal protection.

- Check the title soon after closing (within a couple weeks) to ensure that everything is in order and has been properly recorded. Ask a different title company for validation, instead of the title company that closed the transaction.

A month or so later, the investor was contacted by yet another buyer claiming to have purchased the property and secured a mortgage. This buyer actually closed on the deal, obtained the mortgage, and paid for the property.

After some research and assistance from law enforcement, it was discovered that the seller was involved with a con artist, who acted as the ringleader. The ringleader and the cooperative seller ended up selling the house three times:

1. The first buyer never closed on the transaction, so the buyer lost the house but was not out any money.
2. The second buyer, the investor, paid for the house and took legal possession of it, so he kept the house.

3. The third buyer bought the house and borrowed money to pay for it. He was now facing the painful prospect of paying monthly mortgage payments on a house he didn't own.

The ringleader, 21 years old at the time, planned to use the money from the first sale to go to college. He told the seller that he would handle everything and invest the profits to make the seller even more money. The ringleader never invested the money or returned it to the seller. He did, however, lead the seller to another sale (with the third buyer) in which he offered to split the proceeds with the seller.

In chapter 21, we recommend some changes to the way titles and other documents are recorded that may help cut down on the incidence of double-sales scams or at least make these scams a little more difficult to execute.

9

BUILDER BAILOUTS AND CONTRACTOR CONS:

Dream Home Nightmares

Building a subdivision can be an expensive proposition, especially if the homes don't sell quickly enough. Developers may become buried in bills from subcontractors and suppliers. Payments on high-interest construction loans also start backing up. Facing financial ruin, builders sometimes try to finance their way through the delays by selling homes before they're completed and obtaining conventional mortgages. Often this isn't enough to avoid catastrophe, and buyers, expecting to move into their dream homes, are left with vacant lots, empty bank accounts, and huge mortgages.

And that's assuming the builder is legitimate.

Homeowners may end up in even worse shape if they happen to cross paths with a contractor con artist. A contractor can show up at your house, sell you on the idea of making costly repairs, help you secure the financing to pay for them, and then have the cash sent directly to him. You don't see the money, you don't receive the service, and you may even lose your home. Not only does the shyster have your money, he also has a lien on the property, and if you can't or won't make the payments, he gets to cash out by foreclosing on your home!

This chapter features two stunning cases of builder bailouts and contractor cons along with analyses and postmortems showing what the homeowners should have done.

BUILDER BAILOUTS

Builders often get overextended. Costs for a particular project may exceed estimates, demand for housing declines, or builders overcommit, taking on more projects than they can handle. These situations more commonly arise when the economy is in a slump or interest rates are on the rise, although they can happen at any time. Because most construction loans are high-interest, variable-rate loans, financial problems intensify exponentially in a short period of time.

To understand builder bailouts, understanding how builder financing works is essential. When a bank loans money to a builder, it rarely gives the builder all the money at once. The builder takes out a construction loan that makes the money available through an account controlled by the bank. When the builder has expenses to pay, he draws money from that account. The bank generally requires inspections throughout the building process to make sure the house they're investing in is built according to standards. If the property fails inspection, the bank prevents the builder from drawing additional money from the construction loan account.

Builders may get themselves in a jam if they can't sell a house because it isn't finished, and they can't finish the house because they can't draw money from the construction loan. Desperate builders often resort to some of the following desperate measures to dig themselves out of the hole:

- They falsify construction inspections by submitting fake certifications of work completed.

- They pay off the inspectors to approve additional construction draws.
- They fool the inspectors. In one case, a contractor removed installed items, such as water heaters, from one house to another to pass inspections.
- They sell an unfinished home to a buyer. If the builder goes belly-up, the buyer ends up with mortgage payments on a house that's not finished, along with additional expenses to complete the work.

Once a builder starts to feel a financial pinch, the problem typically snowballs. The builder draws against uncompleted work, reducing the loan balance to a level that's insufficient for completing construction, so the builder draws against construction on other projects. Once this starts, the contractor seldom catches up. Subcontractors and material suppliers are not paid, and in most states they can place a lien on the property; they're entitled to payment even though the contractor was already paid. If the loan is in the name of the homeowner, the homeowner can be left with liens against the property and insufficient funds to pay liens or complete the construction.

Here's how a classic builder bailout goes down:

1. The builder takes out a construction loan.
2. Houses are not selling or not selling fast enough, perhaps due to economy, poor-quality construction, lack of design appeal, lousy neighborhood, etc.
3. The contractor cannot obtain financing to finish projects and begins to fall behind on payments and on construction.
4. The contractor pressures the buyer (who usually has a contract with the builder to purchase the property on completion) to move ahead with purchasing the property immediately. The builder often tells the buyer that this is the customary way of doing business or offers to make the loan payments until construction is completed.

Spotting the **S**igns

Builder bailouts are easy to fall for due to several reasons. First, when buyers hire a builder, they already place trust in that builder. In addition, buyers are often highly motivated to do whatever it takes to have their new homes finished, even if that requires some creative financing. To avoid falling for a builder bailout, watch for these signs:

- The builder is willing to do anything to sell the property.
- The builder offers to sell you a home when you are barely qualified or unqualified for the loan, or offers to sell you the home with no money down.
- The builder gives you the down payment.
- The contract includes upgrades that the builder never performed so you can qualify for a larger loan and get some cash back at closing.
- The builder offers a silent second mortgage to cover upgrades or the down payment.
- The builder pressures you to obtain your loan even though the house isn't finished.
- The builder rushes you to escrow without allowing you to adequately inspect the home or discourages you from obtaining an independent appraisal or home inspection prior to closing.

5. The buyer applies for a loan to purchase the home. Even though the home is not completed, the builder informs the lender that construction has been completed. (Residential loans are not approved for construction purposes so this is, in itself, fraud.)

6. The appraiser appraises the house "as is" (at the value it would have upon completion), or the builder alters the appraisal to make it appear as though construction has been completed.

7. The lender approves financing on the uncompleted home and hands over the money to the builder (property seller). At this point, the buyer owns an unfinished house and is responsible for making the monthly mortgage payments on the loan.

8. Although the builder may complete construction on the house, in most cases, the builder no longer has any motivation to complete the project and uses the money to finance other projects he's fallen behind on.

9. The buyer is left with an unfinished property but has a loan for the full purchase price. While mechanics' liens placed after closing may be covered by title insurance (depending on the policy), the homeowner will not be entitled to any reduction in the loan amount and will not get any funds to complete the home. In fact, the property will likely be over-encumbered, and the buyer won't be able to borrow more money against the property to complete it. Furthermore, the buyer, by signing a loan application based on the false claim that construction was completed, may be guilty of defrauding the lender.

CASE STUDY 1: BUILDER BAILOUT

During the recession in the 1990s, builder bailouts in Georgia were at an all-time high, and desperate builders were often willing to take drastic measures to save their necks. One builder, about to take a loss on an entire subdivision, contrived an elaborate builder bailout to pull himself out of his tailspin.

The builder sold "homes" to his employees, convincing them of his great new moneymaking idea—the employees would buy the homes, and then the builder would rent them out to cover the mortgage payments. When the builder eventually sold the home to "actual buyers," the employees would receive a portion of the proceeds. This was all a lie. The builder had no intention of ever building the homes.

To execute the scam, the builder falsified financial information for his employees and altered preconstruction appraisals that he said would be used to obtain construction financing. He had the appraisals written up to reflect the completed value of the properties, subject to the properties being completed according to plans and specifications. (These types of appraisals are prepared for homeowners or

Protect Yourself

Builder bailouts are some of the nastiest cons in the business. Often the homeowner is stuck with a worthless piece of property and a 30-year mortgage, completely destroying their dream of homeownership. Protect yourself by taking the following precautions:

- Never purchase a home you haven't seen.

- If the purchase is subject to completion by the builder and the construction loan is in your name, make sure the loan document requires you to sign off on progress before the builder can draw from the account.

- Always hire a home inspector to inspect the home before you move in. This is particularly important in new construction because most homebuyers don't know enough about construction to spot structural or material defects.

- Don't pay for a home that the builder hasn't finished yet, no matter what the builder tells you or promises. Withholding final payment is your only way to motivate the builder to finish and do quality work.

builders who are trying to obtain construction financing, so that the lender will know what the home will be worth after it is built.) The builder removed the checkmark in the "subject to completion" section of the appraisals, so they appeared to be for completed houses and the builder's employees could take out residential mortgages. The builder also replaced the photos of the vacant lots and the floor plans with pictures of completed homes.

Moments before the scheduled closings on the nonexistent, supposedly completed homes, the closing agent closed a bulk lot sale for the purchase of the vacant lots on which those nonexistent homes were to be built. He then closed on the "completed home" purchases for more than 20 times the amount paid for the lots! When the lender proceeded to foreclose on the homes, the lender discovered that the lots were vacant or had only stick framing to mark where the homes were supposed to be.

CONTRACTOR CONS

In the 1997 movie *Traveller,* Bill Paxton plays Bokky, an Irish grifter. One of Bokky's cons is to drive around resealing asphalt driveways. Instead of sealant, Bokky applies used motor oil. He collects his money and the next time it rains, the oil washes right down the gutter.

Some contractor cons are just as bold and basic as the one in *Traveller.* Others are more elaborate. Here are some variations of how a bogus contractor might try to scam an unwary homeowner:

- The contractor demands full payment in advance or a hefty deposit and never shows up.
- The contractor performs shoddy work or fails to complete the job.
- You are charged to repair something that's not broken. Contractor cons often involve work on foundations and attics, which the homeowners can't see.
- You are intentionally presented with a low estimate and then charged significantly more upon completion without ever being informed of potential cost overruns.
- The contractor agrees to perform work for an agreed upon price and then halfway through the project demands extra money to complete it. In one common contractor con, the contractor offers to use leftover asphalt from one job to repave a homeowner's driveway. The workers start the job and then demand hundreds or thousands of dollars more to complete it, or they just paint the driveway black and skip out with the money.
- The contractor offers financing and charges illegal loan origination fees, interest rates, and other fees.
- The contractor inspects the house, often under the guise of a utility employee or building or health inspector, claims a serious defect in the property or a health or safety issue, and claims that immediate and expensive repairs are necessary. In some cases, the con artist damages perfectly good equipment (such as a

Spotting the **S**igns

Most homeowners are highly motivated to keep their homes in good repair and are vulnerable to falling for contractor cons. To avoid falling victim to contractor cons, keep an eye out for the following warning signs:

- Contractors who demand payment in full before starting work
- An estimate that is way below what other contractors have estimated
- Free inspections, especially in areas you can't inspect yourself, such as beneath the house or in the attic
- Any home repair offer that is good only for a limited time or will expire if you don't act on it immediately

furnace or air conditioner) and then charges to fix it. In other cases, he simply fines the homeowner for a code violation.

Contractor cons often target senior citizens because they own their own homes, live in older homes, and tend to be more trusting. Sometimes a fake work crew will show up, demand a large deposit before they get started, and even drive with the homeowner to the bank to pick up the money. When the homeowner looks the other way, the crew disappears with the loot.

For additional details on contractor cons, visit Homeowners Against Deficient Dwellings at *www.hadd.com.* Another good place to find information about contractor cons is *www.crimcheck.com/fraud/contractor-fraud-scams.htm.*

CASE STUDY 2: CONTRACTOR CON

In St. Louis, a home repair contractor by the name of Thomas Mark Hogan, owner of All-Phase Construction, defrauded homeown-

Protect Yourself

Dealing with contractors can be a real challenge. Most contractors need some money for materials to get started on a project so you have to trust them to a certain point. The trick is to provide the contractor with the resources she needs without handing over your wallet. Here are some suggestions:

- Attach your own agreement to the contractor's contract describing the work to be done, the deadline, and the agreed upon amount. Stipulate that no additional work is to be done without prior written agreement from you. Consider stating that you will issue payments only for completed work. Have the contractor sign the agreement and keep a copy for yourself.

- Place money in a trust account rather than paying it to the contractor.

- Pay for materials yourself. Verify that the materials have been delivered and are satisfactory before paying the bill.

- Require a release of mechanic's lien rights from subcontractors and material suppliers before making payments or issue joint checks (payable to the contractor and subcontractor or supplier).

- Always check workers' credentials and never let anyone into your home without first asking for identification. Representatives of utility companies and reputable businesses will have identification. If you have concerns over identification, look up the company's phone number on the Internet or in the phone book and call to verify the identity of the workers.

- If you agree that work should be done on your home, ask for an estimate in writing and tell the contractor that you'll get back to him.

- When contracting for home repair services, always get a second opinion and written estimates from one or two other companies.

- Get all guarantees in writing.

- Ask for the names of references for contractors and call them.

- If a free home inspector tells you that damage exists, always get a second opinion before you sign a contract or agree to have any repair work done.

ers out of more than $64,000 in cash. Hogan wasn't very subtle about his con. He simply showed up at his customer's house, provided an estimate, and then demanded payment up front. Once the check cleared, he saw no need to complete the work as promised.

Hogan was hauled into court on an eight-count felony indictment charging him with criminally defrauding his customers. He was ordered to repay $64,133 in restitution to 11 of the homeowners he defrauded and was given a suspended sentence and placed on probation for five years. According to the latest reports from the court, Hogan had paid only $800 in restitution.

10

CHUNKING:

Scamming Eager Investors

Eager, some might say greedy, investors are often prime targets for con artists perpetrating what's commonly called a *chunking* scheme. The con artist pitches an attractive investment scheme, promising anyone who's willing to listen (sometimes an individual and sometimes a roomful of prospective investors) that they will be the proud owners of investment properties and that the con artist will take care of all the details—obtaining the mortgage, placing renters, making the mortgage payments, and so on. Investors are told that the rental payments will cover the mortgage and perhaps generate a little extra cash each month and that investors will make money when the homes are sold.

Unbeknownst to the investor, the properties are typically overvalued, the renters are nonexistent, and the con artist never even makes the mortgage payments. Investors are left with dilapidated homes, unpaid mortgages, and destroyed credit. This chapter dives a little deeper into chunking, features a case study from a young lady who fell victim to a chunking scheme, and offers tips on how you can avoid becoming a victim of or an accomplice in a chunking scheme.

DECONSTRUCTING CHUNKING SCHEMES

The key to a chunking scheme's success is the con artist's ability to make real estate investing seem easy. The con artist promises to handle everything—buy the house, fix it up, find renters, and manage the property (collect the rent, maintain the property, make the mortgage payments, and so on). All you have to do is sign on the dotted line and count your money. To an eager investor, chunking seems like hassle-free real estate investing at its best.

To execute the scam, the con artist needs only two things—a house and a sucker.

To get the house, the con artist prowls the market for distressed properties, including foreclosures, abandoned homes, and new homes that a builder can't sell. The homes don't have to be inhabitable or even pretty because the investor will probably never see the property. The houses just need to be cheap and have an address and some paperwork to verify their existence.

Once the con artist acquires a property, she can start looking for a mark—a sucker to buy the property. The con artist essentially morphs from a homebuyer into a stalker, looking for eager investors who have lots of money or great credit—people who can easily qualify for a loan without drawing suspicion from lenders. To find a mark, the con artist may employ any of several strategies:

- Run an ad on late-night TV promoting a legitimate way to earn thousands of dollars a month investing in real estate
- Post an ad in the classifieds or on the Internet on sites like craigslist
- Stage a seminar for investors
- Sucker a "friend" into investing
- Infiltrate an organization and pitch the scheme to members—a technique referred to as *affinity fraud*

The con artist then obtains an inflated appraisal to make the property look like a valuable piece of real estate—on paper. To convince the investor to buy the house without looking at it, the con artist employs several clever tactics, such as telling investors that they must buy now otherwise another investor will scoop up the property. The con artist may also tell investors that people are currently renting the property: "If you disturb the tenants, you're likely to drive them out. As the new landlord, surely you don't want to do *that!*"

In many cases, the con artist sells multiple properties to a single investor. We've seen cases in which a single investor purchased 98 properties. He thought he was only buying 3 properties, but the con artist took the liberty to use the investor's personal information and financial records to apply for loans to buy the other 95 properties.

The loans are closed within a short period of time so that they will not appear on the buyer's credit report, and the lender won't know that the borrower is buying multiple homes, which would compromise the loan approvals. Frequently, the con artist alters the borrower's financial information and produces phony records to enable the buyer to qualify for the loans. The inflated appraisal also expedites loan approval, making the lender think that the collateral for the loan is more valuable than it really is. To further grease the wheels of the loan approval process, the loan application usually claims that the home will be "owner occupied," so it looks as though the person buying the property will be living there.

The con artist does nothing to rehab the properties, find tenants, or even make the monthly mortgage payments on the property. Because all mortgage statements are mailed directly to the con artist, the investor doesn't know that the payments aren't being made until the properties are in serious default. By the time the investor suspects that something is amiss and finally visits the property, the situation is too far gone. The property is in terrible condition, nobody will rent it, and the investor has no money to fix it up and sell it. The loan goes into default, the lender forecloses, and the investor's credit is destroyed.

The con artist made her money when she flipped the property—buy low, sell high. Sometimes, the con artist wrings a little more money out of the deal by charging the investor remodeling, assignment, or other fees. Practitioners of chunking schemes often justify their actions by

Spotting the **S**igns

As with most scams, chunking schemes prey on those who are most eager and trusting. The con artists who practice chunking are often very likeable people, so never let down your guard, even if your closest "friend" is pitching such a scheme. Keep your eye out for the following warning signs:

- Promises of no-risk, no-effort riches in real estate. Real estate investing can be profitable, but it requires hard work and vigilance.

- Any pressure or attempt to get you to purchase property without seeing it or inspecting it first

- Any attempt to get you to forgo an independent appraisal in favor of one supplied by the real estate agent, loan officer, seller, or person who is arranging the sale

- Pressure to use a particular title company

- Claims that lenders will allow you to close on multiple investment properties back-to-back without disclosing the prior or concurrent purchases

- A sudden change of seller at closing. When you think you're buying the property from someone, and the name of that someone mysteriously changes on the closing papers, watch out.

- Two closings on the same property have to occur in close succession. For example, the person you're buying the property from is buying and closing on that same property only a short time prior to your purchase of it.

claiming that they were just living the American dream and being savvy capitalists: "If the investor didn't investigate the value of the property or even look at it before he purchased it, how can that be my fault?"

CASE STUDY

Debbie Yack, a hardworking young lady, can tell you all about the risks of chunking schemes. She was personally sucked into such a scheme by a con artist who befriended her and then sold her the bill of goods. Yack has generously offered to share her story here in the hopes of helping others avoid similar scams:

"I was scammed by one of my friends, a mortgage broker who, needless to say, is no longer my friend. On November 1, 2005, I was getting laid off from my full-time job and needed another source of income.

"My friend approached with what sounded like the deal of a lifetime. He had a house for sale for $120,000. The previous owner was in foreclosure. I would own the house for only one year. In the meantime, the previous owner would pay me rent and work on rebuilding her credit, so she could buy the house back from me at the end of the year for more than I had paid for it.

"I told my friend that I didn't think that I would get approved for a loan because I would only be working part-time at TGI Fridays and collecting unemployment. He told me that wouldn't be a problem at all. He was right. Supposedly, the loan approval was based entirely on my good credit score, so I was able to buy the house for $120,000, and I didn't even have a put any money down. After the closing, my friend gave me $8,300 in cash and told me that I could use the money just in case my renter was unable to pay the monthly rent. If she paid the rent, I could keep the extra money.

"Two weeks later, my friend called and told me he had another home for me to buy—a duplex that already had two renters and was selling for $208,150. The deal was pretty similar to the first one—the tenants would pay me monthly rent for about a year while my friend tried to sell the property for more than I had paid for it. I bought the duplex. At closing, I received $5,000 in cash just in case my renters didn't pay their rent.

"I told another one of my friends what I was doing. He was shocked that I was able to buy two houses and get cash back at closing while I was receiving unemployment. He wanted to do the same thing. He wanted in. I called my mortgage broker and set up a meeting between his group and my friend, but the group didn't want my friend as an investor because they didn't know enough about him.

"After being rejected, my friend did a little research and found out that I had been involved in mortgage fraud. He told me I should never have received cash back when I bought the houses and that my loan application should never have been approved because I was collecting unemployment and had no money for a down payment.

"I immediately went down to the FBI office in downtown Detroit and filed a report. I came clean. I told them everything I did and everything this mortgage broker did. They told me I had to follow up with the White Collar Unit. Days later, I contacted an agent from the White Collar Unit, and she told me there was nothing the FBI could do for me because my homes were not in foreclosure. The FBI simply had too many mortgage fraud cases to investigate that were already in foreclosure.

"Finally, one of my friends told me about Ralph Roberts and his website *FlippingFrenzy.com*. I called Ralph and set up a meeting, during which Ralph explained how real estate and mortgage fraud work. After that meeting, I kept getting phone calls from my mortgage broker friend telling me that he had another property that he wanted me to buy. I told him that I wasn't interested in buying any more homes. He didn't know that I knew what he was doing was fraud. And he didn't know that I had talked to Ralph and the FBI.

"One day, my mortgage broker friend called me again and told me that he had me cleared to close on another home. I found out the name of the lender and called that bank to put a stop to the loan. The brokers, including my 'friend,' learned that I had put a stop to the loan, and they showed up that night at my rental unit extremely perturbed.

Protect Yourself

Chunking schemes prey on vulnerable people who typically have excellent credit, but as you can see from Yack's story, con artists can work around a poor credit rating. Anyone who's not careful is a potential mark. To protect yourself, remain vigilant and take these necessary precautions:

- Always inspect a property with your own two eyes before buying it. Your real estate agent can contact tenants and arrange visits so don't accept the possibility of inconveniencing tenants or any other reason to convince you to forgo personally visiting the property. Make sure that you obtain access to and inspect every unit in a multiunit rental.

- If an opportunity sounds too good to be true, it probably is. Consult a real estate attorney in your area to see what she thinks.

- Don't rush into a deal just because someone says the deal won't last another minute. Investment property is always readily available, and if you miss out on one opportunity, you can find others.

- Obtain an independent appraisal before closing. Don't let the seller or the seller's representative tell you which appraiser to use—pick your own.

- Obtain an independent home inspection before closing. This is a good time to visit the property yourself, if you haven't done so already.

- Steer clear of get-rich-quick real estate seminars and websites or at least investigate them before becoming involved.

They were beginning to realize that the gig was up, and I was beginning to realize just how much of a hassle this no-hassle real estate investing really was.

"To protect myself, I had to take immediate action. I drove down to the local police station and filed an identity theft report, because the brokers had submitted a loan application in my name without my permission. I called the credit reporting agency and added a fraud alert to my credit report. I called the Social Security Fraud hotline because these scammers had my Social Security number. I also had to file a report with the Federal Trade Commission.

"I have now hired an attorney to try and sort out this mess.

"Every couple of weeks, I send my contact at the FBI a letter, telling her the new developments in the case, but, as of January 18, 2007, I haven't heard from her.

"I am fighting an endless war on my own. In the meantime, I am going through two foreclosures and my credit is ruined.

"I consider myself a very honest person, and I would never intentionally do anything even remotely considered illegal or immoral. I signed documents without the slightest hesitation because I trusted my friend, a real estate professional, to do the right thing and to do what was in my best interest. Now I am paying the price for trusting that person."

To learn more about spotting the warning signs of sham real estate investment seminars, visit *www.johntreed.com/reedgururating.html*.

11

PONZI SCHEMES AND PYRAMIDS:

Floating Funny Money

You're disappointed by the performance of your stocks and bonds. You'd like to invest in real estate, but you don't want the hassles of owning and maintaining a property. You'd rather put up the money and have someone else handle the details. Along comes a professional real estate investor who presents the opportunity you've been looking for. He offers to sell you secured loans that promise guaranteed, double-digit returns. Watch your wallet. This smooth-talking investor may be targeting you for one of the oldest scams in the books—a Ponzi scheme.

Pyramid schemes are a little more obvious. The ringleader simply turns you into a recruiter of recruiters and requests a relatively small initial investment with the promise of a big payday when all the people you recruited pay their dues.

In this chapter, we expose Ponzi and pyramid schemes for what they really are—big rip-offs—and then show you how to spot the signs and protect yourself from falling victim to them.

WHAT ARE PONZI AND PYRAMID SCHEMES?

Ponzi and pyramid schemes are classic "too good to be true" scams. Although they differ in theory and execution, the underlying similarity is that in both types of schemes, the promised return on investment is paid out of money collected from people who enroll in the program later, assuming any return on the investment is ever paid. Due to the nature of Ponzi and pyramid schemes, all of them are destined to collapse, but not before the ringleaders collect their money.

Ponzi Schemes

Ponzi schemes are named for Carlo "Charles" Ponzi, a Massachusetts get-rich-quick entrepreneur who offered a 50-percent return on investments in postal coupons during the 1920s. As in modern day Ponzi schemes, he was able to pay initial investors the guaranteed return only by conning more money out of new investors. Eventually, he reached a point at which he was unable to find enough new investors to pay off existing investors, and the scheme collapsed—which is what always happens in a Ponzi scheme.

Ponzi schemes are usually structured as investment opportunities. The ringleader offers interest in a real estate company or sells second trust deeds against properties (sometimes even first trust deeds). When using trust deeds, the ringleader typically pulls together a group of investors who contribute to a pool to fund second liens (second mortgages) against real property.

Of course, second mortgages are far riskier than first-position mortgages because foreclosure or liquidation often preserves the first lien position while wiping out the second lien. In addition, when homeowners face financial setbacks, they often make their first mortgage payments and ignore payments on second mortgages because second lien holders are less likely to move quickly to foreclosure, especially if the owners have little to no equity in the property. In other words, although the ringleader or recruiter is promising a low-risk,

A*ffinity* F*raud*

Ponzi and pyramid schemes often involve *affinity fraud*. With affinity fraud, the ringleader or recruiter targets a group that she belongs to, earns the trust of the group's members, and then uses that trust to con them out of their money. Perpetrators of affinity fraud pursue identifiable groups of people such as church members, racial or ethnic groups, and real estate investment groups. Because the person is a member of the group, the group typically lets down its guard and is more likely to fall for whatever deal the ringleader or recruiter is pitching.

high-return investment opportunity, the investments are often very risky—the promise of "guaranteed" returns is an empty promise.

The people who organize these schemes are usually smooth talkers. They're often well-respected businesspeople in their community—many have had other successful businesses or even operated real estate companies or real estate investment companies for several years. They allay all the fears of their marks and explain away all the inconsistencies inherent in the schemes. Many claim they believed in their ideas and had a sincere intent to make their investors rich.

Ponzi schemes are set to implode from the second they are launched, but the causes of implosion may vary. In most cases, the investments simply don't perform as promised so the ringleader uses the money from new investors to pay the old investors. This quickly leads to ruin because the ringleader runs out of capital to finance new investments. We've seen cases in which the ringleaders get very creative with notary and recording stamps, creating false deeds to provide proof of investment to incoming investors whose money is essentially being stolen.

In some cases, a legitimate investment pool morphs into a Ponzi scheme due to the pride of the ringleader. Rather than inform investors that a particular trust deed or pool of trust deeds has performed poorly or lost money, the ringleader continues to pay investors their "guaranteed" returns. After all, if the investment doesn't perform well, the investors may drop out. These scenarios typically occur when the ringleader has an eternal sense of optimism. Believing that they can make up the shortfall on the next deal, the ringleaders dig themselves (and their investors) into an ever deepening hole. Despite the fact that they are keeping four different sets of books, soliciting new investors so they can keep paying old investors, and juggling investments to make it appear that their promises are being fulfilled, they usually believe that they'll be able to pull out of the tailspin—right up until the time that the FBI knocks on their doors.

In the worst cases, the scheme is intentionally designed to fleece investors. Ringleaders purchase no property or trust deeds. They provide only phony documentation. These ringleaders are the true snake-oil salesmen, making grandiose promises to little old ladies in order to steal their life savings and use the cash to fund their lavish lifestyles. When they can no longer placate investors with tales of delayed payments and can't obtain enough money from new investors to keep the creditors at bay, they fold up operations and move on to another town, another scheme, another set of victims.

Pyramid Schemes

Pyramid schemes are a little less sinister in nature because everyone involved knows up front what's going on. The classic scheme is the chain letter that instructs you to give a dollar to the sender, move the top name off the list, add your name to the bottom, and send the letter to 10 other recipients, instructing them to repeat the process. Each time this happens, your name moves up one notch on the list. Theoretically, when the letter reaches its 10th iteration, your name is at the top of the list and each of the 10,000,000,000 recipients who now have a letter with your name at the top each sends you a dollar. It's a great idea for the first name on the list, but many people don't respond, and later participants just lose their money.

Spotting the Signs

Of course, Ponzi and pyramid schemes aren't always so easy to spot because ringleaders have devised all sorts of clever ways to pitch these arrangements. The warning flags, however, are fairly standard:

- Promises of guaranteed high returns and no risk
- High-energy and excited sales pitches with little to no real information
- Highly intricate and complicated investment opportunities that are difficult to understand
- Ringleaders who discourage you from obtaining independent advice and encourage you to consult with their advisors
- Ringleaders who rely on your trust or common interests in the community to get you to invest money
- Investments that start small and then require larger and larger capital influxes, especially as returns start to slow
- Promises of limitless income
- No product or service being sold or a product being sold for far more than it's worth
- Promised income is primarily from commissions or influx of investments from new members

Pyramid schemes work pretty much the same way in real estate. In at least one instance, the pyramid arrangement was used to pull off a mortgage elimination scam (see chapter 16). Ringleaders encouraged homeowners to sign up and make a $3,000 payment to contribute to paying off the mortgages of other people who entered the program previously. Eventually, later enrollees would pay off your mortgage, and you'd end up owning your house for a mere $3,000 one-time payment! Of course, none of the money received was used to pay off a single mortgage. It went directly into the pockets of the ringleaders.

Protect **Y**ourself

Ponzi and pyramid schemes make big, empty promises so the trick to protecting yourself is to avoid falling for pumped-up promises of no-risk investments with high returns:

- Don't believe operators who promise quick, no-risk, no-hassle riches in real estate. If an investment sounds too good to be true, it probably is. If the deal is really so great, why does the person pitching it need your money?

- Remain suspicious of ostentatious wealth. A ringleader's gold rings, fancy car, and mansion are no indication of the viability of the product or system she's pitching. These symbols of wealth may simply prove that the person is good at ripping off people.

- Avoid any investment opportunities you don't completely understand. Ringleaders intentionally make schemes complicated so that investors are more likely to hand over their money, no questions asked.

- Consult an independent accountant or financial advisor to review the prospectus. Don't accept a referral from the ringleader, and be very suspicious of anyone who tries to discourage you from seeking independent review or tries to steer you to an advisor, especially if they tell you that you should just "trust" them.

- Research the ringleaders through government regulators, including the Securities and Exchange Commission (SEC), the Federal Trade Commission (FTC), and industry trade groups.

- Run the name of the investment and the ringleaders through Google and on investment chat boards to see if other people are talking about them. You won't always find something, but when these schemes start to collapse, the victims generally start talking and posting their concerns on the Internet. It's at these times that the ringleaders begin desperately seeking new investors.

- Educate yourself. If you are going to invest in unregistered securities, at least know the minimum disclosures and investor requirements. Don't invest your money with operations that are not complying with government regulations.

The problem with all pyramid schemes is that they are mathematically unsustainable. Take the chain letter example. By the time that the 10th letter is sent out, 10 million people must be involved in order for the last person to obtain the promised benefit. The mathematical progression of these schemes quickly requires participation by the entire nation and then the entire world's population!

CASE STUDY

July 11, 2006, Santa Cruz, California: According to court reports, Michael J. Schneider, owner and operator of California Plan, Inc., managed to con investors who believed they were making secured real estate loans out of more than $17.5 million. Both Schneider and California Plan, Inc. were licensed by the Department of Real Estate as mortgage brokers.

Schneider's scam is an example of the most brazen form of Ponzi schemes. Schneider led investors to believe that they were making loans secured with validly recorded deeds of trust, but in most cases, authorities allege he was simply taking the investors' money and providing them with phony deeds of trust. In cases in which he did secure the loan with a valid deed, when the loan was paid off, Schneider allegedly simply pocketed the money rather than paying the investor. To avoid suspicion, Schneider sent monthly payments to investors, financed with the proceeds from new investors.

12

MANUFACTURED HOUSING SCAMS

A home on wheels is an easy target. Manufactured housing scams include not only the elements of real estate fraud but also those associated with vehicle fraud. From bait-and-switch scams to overnight subdivisions with inflated values, this segment of the market experiences a significant amount of fraudulent schemes. The most ambitious con artists can build and sell an entire run-down subdivision in a matter of days. This chapter reveals the devastating results of manufactured housing scams, relates an actual case study, and explores the warning signs that buyers need to be aware of.

IDENTIFYING THE TOOLS OF MANUFACTURED HOUSING CON ARTISTS

Manufactured housing is marketed as affordable housing primarily to low-income families and the elderly. For a fraction of the price of a new home built on a lot that the buyer owns, you can purchase a prebuilt model that you can "park" on any lot of your choosing. Sound attractive? For some homeowners, manufactured housing is the only option they can afford short of renting, but manufactured housing has several drawbacks:

- Like a car, a manufactured house automatically depreciates significantly as soon as you "drive" it off the lot.
- Manufactured houses rarely if ever appreciate. Don't expect to be able to sell the home for more than you paid for it. You'll usually take a loss when you sell.
- The cost of the house rarely includes other amenities, such as lot rental or purchase, transport costs, and additional features. These are often sold as add-ons, like vehicle options when you buy a car.

Unfortunately, the drawbacks inherent in manufactured housing aren't the only disadvantages. Con artists often prey on those who are attracted to manufactured housing simply because they are generally more vulnerable and because the mobility of the housing makes these scams particularly easy to execute.

The following sections highlight the most popular scams that target buyers of manufactured housing.

The Old Bait-and-Switch Con

The old bait-and-switch maneuver is a common marketing tactic. Think back to the last time you bought a package of hamburger meat. You thought you were purchasing fresh, red hamburger, but when you dug down, you discovered that the meat in the middle was the old, gray stuff.

Some dealers who sell manufactured housing pull the same types of scams on unwary buyers. Following is a description of a shady sales practice followed by a description of an outright scam. The most common scams include the following:

- *Automatic upgrades.* The dealer places an ad for a used or repossessed home. The buyers show up, purchase the home, complete a credit application, and are notified that they qualify for financing. At closing, the homeowners are sold a newly manufactured home with a much higher price tag.
- *Used home at a new price.* The dealer shows the buyers a newly manufactured home, leads them to believe that this is the home they're buying, and then delivers a used home in its place, complete with all the problems you would expect to find in a used model. Having sold the home at full price, the dealer gets to pocket the difference between the value of the used home and the value of the new home.

The treatment of manufactured homes varies from state to state. In some states, the home is considered part of the land—real estate. Other states treat manufactured homes as personal property, like a car. These issues can affect both the sale and the buyers' legal rights if they seek restitution.

Inflated Home Values

Inflated appraisals can generate risky loans on any type of home, but appraisals on manufactured housing are particularly vulnerable to inflation. How much is a manufactured house worth? That's a tricky question. In addition to the purchase price, appraisers often include the following costs in their estimates:

- Delivery costs
- Installation costs

These costs can't be recouped when the homeowner sells the property, and because the property quickly depreciates as soon as it leaves the lot, the lender often approves a loan for significantly more than the house is worth. If the homeowners experience a financial setback,

Spotting the Signs

If you're in the market for a manufactured home, learn to recognize the signs of shady deals and outright cons:

- Mistakes in your contract regarding the type, make, model, size, or other details of the manufactured home you intend to purchase

- Delivery dates that are continually pushed back

- Salespeople who try to falsify your income or other personal details or recommend that you fudge the facts to obtain loan approval

- A salesperson who refuses to give you copies of the contracts or loan documents

- A salesperson who offers to put incorrect sales price information on the contract or makes some other adjustments so you don't have to make the down payment that the lender requires

- A higher sales price at closing than the agreed upon amount, incorporating higher fees, additional costs, higher interest, or add-ons for items that you were told were included in the sales price

they usually have negative equity in the property and have no financial buffer to get them through the hard times. If the home's value was inflated at the time of purchase, the problem is even worse.

Creating Ghost Town Subdivisions

Buy a piece of property in a rural area; subdivide it into small lots; place a manufactured home on each lot; add some front steps, a driveway, and some landscaping; and voilà, you have an instant new subdivision. Put a couple of the units into escrow to use as comparable sales for appraisals on other lots, market the homes with no down payment required to low-income buyers with poor credit, and you can make millions! Con artists do it all the time.

These subdivisions sell out quickly. Sometimes, the con artists sell to straw buyers—fictional buyers or unfortunate parties who've been conned into believing that they were taking loans out to finance a valuable real estate investment. Frequently, the con artists simply sell the units to real families looking for affordable housing.

These manufactured subdivisions are often abandoned in less time than was required to sell them. The homes may not even have standard plumbing—the sewage lines are directed to a leach field or drainage ditch shared by 20 or more units. The new owners can't make the payments and can't sell, so the lenders are left taking possession of an entire subdivision of homes that are deserted, boarded up, and worthless.

CASE STUDY

North Carolina was home to one of the most sinister and audacious manufactured housing scams in the nation. Fortunately, the perpetrators were caught and convicted, forced to forfeit all their property, pay restitution of more than $7 million, and serve five years of probation.

The mastermind of the operation was a guy named Donald Gupton. He owned a manufactured home sales lot in Vance County, North Carolina. Gupton and his accomplice, one of Gupton's employees, engaged in a scheme to sell manufactured homes to unqualified buyers. To qualify buyers for loans, Gupton's group pulled every mortgage fraud trick in the book:

- The down payment information was falsified to make the loan applicant appear to have a lower debt-to-income ratio.
- The title was conveyed without transferring possession of a manufactured home to make it appear as though the applicant was trading one home for another at closing rather than buying a new home. (The same manufactured home was used as a trade-in for nine different homebuyers.)

Protect **Y**ourself

Manufactured housing scams are all too easy to execute, and they target the most vulnerable buyers. To prevent yourself from falling victim to such scams, take the appropriate preventive measures:

- Always double-check your contract to ensure the details are accurate and the delivery date is specified.

- Make sure that all of the promises the dealer made are in the written contract.

- Make sure the contract has a solid conditional clause that gives you an absolute legal right to cancel the contract and get your money back if the company doesn't deliver the home you ordered on the promised date.

- Object to any creative financing maneuvers intended to provide you with cash back at closing or to forgo the lender's requirement for a down payment.

- Don't accept delivery of the home until after you've verified the make, model, year, and size of the home and other details against your contract.

- Don't accept delivery of a home that's different from what you expected or paid for.

- Always obtain a copy of everything you sign.

- Falsified documents were notarized with Gupton's employees acting as notaries.
- A phony gift letter from the buyer's relative was prepared and the buyer was instructed to have her relative sign the letter so it looked as though the buyer was receiving a cash gift sufficient to cover the down payment.
- Buyers were provided cash to deposit in their accounts and then they returned the money after receiving loan approval.
- Manufactured home invoices were fabricated to make the homes appear more valuable than they really were so buyers could obtain approval for larger loan amounts.

- Land sale contracts were fabricated to use as down payments and demonstrate that the buyers had a vested interest in the property. In most cases, the land didn't exist or Gupton didn't own it as he had claimed, and the buyers were not making payments on the contract.

In a matter of four years, Gupton and company managed to sell over 150 manufactured homes for a gross sales total of more than $11 million. All of these were HUD-backed mortgages, so both lenders and taxpayers were being duped into making risky loans, and buyers were usually setting themselves up for financial failure. The only winners in this scheme were Gupton and his cohorts, and, fortunately, the law caught up with them.

13

LEASE OPTION AND LAND SALE CONTRACTS:

The Unrecorded Deals

Lease option and land sale contracts provide a legitimate way to convey ownership of a property, but con artists often use them to rip off homeowners and fleece buyers. The con artist may sell the house using an illusory lease option agreement, refuse to honor the option, and then evict the tenant, leaving the potential buyers without a home and without their initial deposit and monthly payments. These arrangements are also used in the double-sales scams for investment properties, in which the con artist sells to one person and then sells to another on a land sale contract. Because the land sale contracts aren't recorded and title doesn't transfer until the entire price has been paid, the fraudster has sold the property, received full value, and still receives payments every month on the land sale contract.

This chapter explains the pros and cons of lease option and land sale contracts, demonstrates how con artists abuse them to take advantage of vulnerable homeowners and buyers, reveals the warning signs you need to watch out for, and shows you how to protect yourself from becoming the next victim.

UNDERSTANDING LEASE OPTION AND LAND SALE CONTRACT SCAMS

Lease option and land sale contracts are legitimate means to buy and sell real estate. They enable buyers and homeowners to purchase or buy back properties or transfer ownership when conditions aren't quite right for them to do so immediately. Before exploring the scams in which lease option and land sale contracts are used illegitimately, you need to understand how these vehicles are used legitimately in real estate transactions:

- *Lease option.* Instead of purchasing the property outright, under a lease option agreement, the buyer rents the property for a certain period and has an option to purchase the property either during or at the end of the rental period. Usually the buyer under a lease option is required to make a one time lump-sum payment to the seller to "buy" the option—the right to purchase at a certain price at a future date. Sometimes the monthly payments on a lease option are set higher than market rent, with a portion of the monthly payment applied to the purchase price. A lease option can be a great deal for someone who wants to purchase a property immediately and can't qualify for financing but will be able to qualify in the foreseeable future.
- *Land sale contract.* A land sale contract is a rent-to-own agreement that provides another way for a buyer to purchase a property without having to qualify for a loan. The seller agrees to sell the property to the buyer on contract and holds the title of the property until the buyer has paid for the property in full. A land sale contract typically has a forfeiture provision stating that if the buyer misses a payment or the payment is late, the sale is terminated and the seller retains possession of the property and gets to keep all payments. This is a perfectly legitimate way to buy and sell properties in some states, as long as the seller doesn't abuse her rights.

Lease Options: Win-Win Transactions

A lease option deal can be a win-win situation for both parties—the buyer and the seller. The buyer can lock in the purchase price of a home in an area where home values are on the rise. For example, if you have a lease option to buy a home for $250,000 over the course of 24 months and the home increases in value by 10 percent over that two-year period, you have $25,000 of equity built up in the house. This can help you obtain a conventional loan to purchase the property or you can use it as a down payment on the property when you exercise your option to buy the house.

The seller benefits by obtaining tenants who will treat the house with tender loving care because they're planning on eventually owning the property. The seller has less property maintenance to perform, usually collects a nonrefundable option fee up front (with a deferred tax), has a steady cash flow from the monthly rent, and has a buyer lined up to purchase the property when the lease option term expires. In addition, instead of paying short-term capital gains on profits from the sale of property that is quickly bought and resold(in less than a year's time), the seller can hold the property in excess of a year so the profits qualify for the much lower long-term capital gains tax rate.

Lease Option Scams

Although lease option contracts are legitimate, they're very easy to abuse. In the most blatant cases of abuse, the seller simply refuses to honor the contract. He accepts the nonrefundable lease option deposit, collects the monthly payments, and then simply refuses to sell when the lease term expires. Sometimes the contract is worded in such a way that the buyer has to jump through hoops to comply with the conditions stated in the contract. Failure to comply results in default, and the seller is legally empowered to back out of the contract and keep the payments without completing the sale.

In more subtle cons, the seller targets low-income buyers who have bad credit. The seller is fairly certain that the buyer will never be able to obtain the financing required to ultimately purchase the

Protect Yourself

If you enter into a lease option agreement and the seller tries to evict you for no good reason or refuses to sell when the lease period expires, consult an attorney. As you're making the monthly payments and the property value is increasing (which is the usual scenario), you're building up equity in the property. When the seller refuses to sell or tries to evict you on some technicality, what she's really doing is trying to deprive you of the equity in the property—equity that you worked hard to build.

Some investors believe that this strategy for skimming equity is perfectly legitimate, but it's not. The con artist is simply using a legitimate real estate tool to lend credibility to the scheme. Most people have heard of lease options and rarely hesitate to sign such contracts. Perhaps their grandparents, other family members, or friends have purchased homes via lease option contracts. In the hands of a con artist or ambitious real estate opportunist, however, lease option contracts can be very detrimental to buyers.

property. Real estate infomercials on late-night TV often promote this get-rich-quick strategy. The seller may pitch the deal as a way for the homeowner to purchase a property with no money down. In many cases, the seller offers to help the buyers fix any credit problems they may have during the lease period and then never delivers on that promise. At the end of the lease period, the prospective buyers have the same poor credit they did when they signed the contract and cannot obtain loan approval to purchase the house. The prospective buyers are in no position to buy the property and are evicted, allowing the seller to pitch another lease option deal using the same property to another financially strapped family. The family that originally entered into the deal is even less likely to be in a position to purchase a home in the future because their savings were used to make the nonrefundable option payment and pay the above-market rent.

Lease options are also used as a tool in other types of scams, including the chunking schemes described in chapter 10. The con artist convinces someone to purchase an investment property and promises to take care of everything. The con artist then offers lease option or land contract deals to the property "renters" without informing the investor. This is illegal because the investor is the actual property owner—the only one authorized to enter into such an agreement. The con artist charges more in monthly payments than is required to cover the mortgage payments and simply pockets the difference.

This can be devastating for the "buyers" who enter into the lease option contract. They're making higher payments believing that they are purchasing a home when, in fact, they will never have the opportunity to complete the purchase because the real owner hasn't agreed to the sale. Of course, this rarely happens because the con artist usually targets low-income consumers with credit problems and evicts them when they cannot qualify for a mortgage.

Land Sale Contract Scams

Land sale contracts generally have forfeiture provisions stating that if the buyer misses a payment or even makes one late payment, the land sale contract terminates and the seller keeps all payments up to that point along with the property. These forfeiture provisions generally operate up to the very last payment, resulting in a theoretical situation in which a buyer could make mortgage payments for 30 years and then lose the property by being late on the very last payment.

In some states, these types of contracts are treated like mortgages and the forfeiture provisions are invalid. In these states, the seller is required to foreclose on the property, which provides the homeowner with additional legal options to make good on the loan. Unfortunately, the perpetrators of land sale contract scams often target unsophisticated, low-income families, immigrant communities, and other populations that can't qualify for conventional loans and are reluctant to seek legal counsel. So the perpetrators get away with enforcing the forfeiture provisions even in states where such provisions are not valid.

S*potting the* **S***igns*

Lease option and land sale contracts are common, legitimate vehicles for buying and selling properties so we don't want to discourage you from using these options to purchase a home, but you do need to be careful and remain on the lookout for the following red flags:

- The seller's name on the contract doesn't match the name of the person selling you the property.

- Based on your household income, you're unlikely to be able to make the monthly payments for any length of time.

- On a lease option contract, you're unlikely to be able to qualify for a mortgage loan to buy the property when the lease term expires.

- The seller offers to help you repair your credit so you can obtain a loan to purchase the house when the lease period expires.

- The terms of the contract are confusing or are worded so that you would be hard-pressed to fulfill your obligations.

- The contract is worded in a way that the seller can easily back out of the deal at any time and refuse to sell you the property.

- A land sale contract allows for forfeiture up through the last payment with no return of any of the purchase funds.

CASE STUDY

On March 28, 2000, five tornados touched down in and around Fort Worth, Texas, destroying or severely damaging 70 homes in the Linwood suburb of Fort Worth. The neighborhood was primarily populated by Hispanic, first-time homebuyers who had purchased their homes by way of contracts for deed.

Shortly after the tornado damage, they discovered that, although they considered themselves homeowners, they didn't have the rights or protections that go along with ownership. Many discovered that

Protect Yourself

When you're dealing with a seller who's acting with integrity, a lease option or land sale contract can be a mutually beneficial agreement. Before signing such a contract, however, take some precautions to protect your interests:

- Read and understand all documents before signing them.

- Hire an attorney to review all documents before signing them. Make sure that the purchase and default provisions are fair and that you understand exactly what they state. (When entering an agreement to purchase a property worth tens or hundreds of thousands of dollars, paying an attorney a couple or few hundred dollars is well worth the investment.)

- Make sure that the person selling you the property is the owner and that their name is listed on the contract and on the property's title.

- Close the deal through a reputable title or escrow company. If you're unsure about the company's reputation, call a real estate office in your area and ask.

- Stay informed about the state of title during the term of a land sale contract so that the seller doesn't allow judgments and liens to pile up against the title to the property.

- Make sure that the lease option or land sale contract is recorded against the title to the home. You can contact the county clerk or register of deeds to double-check.

- If the property owner will be responsible for paying property taxes, check with the county tax assessor's department annually to make sure that the tax payments are up to date.

- If the property owner is responsible for paying the insurance premiums, make sure the premiums are being paid and that you're listed as an additional insured on the homeowners' insurance policy.

the property sellers had not maintained insurance for the homes despite the monthly payments the homebuyers made. The residents were also unable to obtain government aid or loans to repair the homes because they weren't owners or renters. Because of the forfeiture provisions in the contracts for deed, the homebuyers were often forced to continue to pay the monthly payments on the homes in order to avoid forfeiture—even though the homes were uninhabitable. They were also paying for hotels or alternative rental housing in order to have somewhere to live.

The damage caused by the tornados brought the problems of contract for deed arrangements into sharp focus in Texas. Subsequent civil lawsuits alleged additional wrongful conduct by property sellers in these situations. As a result, in 2001 Texas passed legislation providing protections for buyers under contracts for deed.

14

STEALING HOUSES WITH TAX DEEDS AND PHONY DEEDS

A stranger shows up at your house and claims to have purchased your home at a tax sale. He shows you the tax deed or certificate he purchased, which looks official, and informs you that he is now the new owner of your home, and you are legally obligated to vacate the premises immediately. What do you do?

You're going through your mail one day, and you discover a foreclosure notice from a bank claiming that you failed to make payments on a particular loan you can't recall ever having applied for. You've been a little forgetful lately, but you couldn't possibly have forgotten something like taking out a second mortgage on your home! You call the bank, and sure enough, even though the bank won't talk to you about the mortgage because it isn't in your name, the address of your property is listed on the mortgage note. How could that possibly have happened? What legal recourse do you have?

Con artists have devised all sorts of clever schemes to steal houses right out from under homeowners and cash out the equity in a home simply by purchasing tax deeds or recording phony deeds. This chapter features three case studies in which con artists abused deeds to rip off homeowners and lenders—either by stealing their homes or borrowing against the property. You will learn how to spot the signs of tax deed and phony deed scams and how to protect yourself from con artists who plan on making you their next victim.

HOW CON ARTISTS USE DEEDS TO STEAL HOMES

Thieves don't have to point a gun at you to steal your money. They can steal much more with a lot less hassle by using a fountain pen. They simply buy a tax deed for pennies on the dollar at a tax sale or head down to your county's register of deeds office and file some phony paperwork showing that you deeded your house over to them.

In the following sections, we explore the various methods that con artists use to steal houses and walk away with the equity that homeowners have worked so hard to build up in their properties.

Tax Deed Scams

When homeowners fail to pay their property taxes, the government typically notifies the homeowners that the taxes are overdue and assesses a late-payment penalty. The government also charges interest on back taxes. Homeowners usually pay the back taxes, penalties, and interest, but if the homeowners are ill or not currently residing at the address, they may not receive the notice until it's too late. The government then places a tax lien on the property, and after some time may sell the property or the tax lien at a public tax sale.

The process by which properties are sold by the government varies from state to state. All states hold public tax sales, but some states actually sell the property and convey title by way of a tax deed, while others sell the tax lien itself and provide the high bidder with a tax lien certificate. These processes are as follows:

- *Tax deed states.* In tax deed states, the buyer purchases the property itself and the government provides the buyer with a tax deed. Because property tax liens take priority over all other liens against the property, such as first and second mortgage liens, the buyer obtains a deed that's free and clear of any other liens. In some states, the homeowners who failed to pay their taxes have a redemption period—a certain amount of time to pay the back taxes and interest to the person who purchased the tax deed. In states without a redemption period, the person who received the tax deed immediately becomes the legal owner of the property.

- *Tax lien certificate states.* Instead of auctioning off the title to a home, some states auction off the tax lien by transferring what is called a *tax lien certificate.* The winning bidder pays the amount of the bid (usually equal to or higher than the amount of taxes owed) and receives the tax lien certificate. The homeowners can choose to redeem the tax lien by paying the high bidder the back taxes plus interest. If the homeowners fail to redeem within the set time period, the holder of the tax lien certificate has the right to foreclose on the property and obtain title to the home. The key point with tax lien certificates is that they do not actually transfer title to the property even though the high bidder purchased the lien. The homeowners retain the right, through a statutory time period, to pay off the lien plus interest and keep the home.

In one type of scam, the holder of the tax lien certificate approaches the homeowner and states that they have purchased the home and the homeowner must move out or must execute a quitclaim deed or other type of deed that transfers ownership of the property to the certificate holder. This is not true, but many homeowners fall for this ploy because they're unaware of their redemption rights. They truly believe that they have lost their home due to some legal technicality.

The purchaser would not legally be entitled to bring a lawsuit and evict the homeowners because the purchaser doesn't actually own the property. Of course, if the homeowner signs a deed, this results in an immediate transfer of ownership. The take-home message here is this: If someone shows up at your house with a tax deed or tax lien certificate claiming ownership or other rights to your property, don't sign anything. Consult an attorney immediately.

In most cases, tax-certificate cons target homeowners who have few or no other liens against the property so when they take ownership, they don't have to pay off those other liens. Honest investors typically hold the tax lien certificate until they can legally foreclose on the property because the foreclosure process extinguishes all other liens.

Forged Deeds

More and more con artists are simply stealing houses right out from under the homeowners by recording forged deeds that transfer ownership of the property to the con artist or some intermediary player. These con artists typically target vacant properties, vacation homes, or elderly homeowners. We often see this occur in situations in which the elderly owners have entered nursing facilities or have extended hospital stays.

Here's how the perpetrators typically pull off these phony deed scams:

1. The con artist forges the homeowner's name on a deed and then records the deed in the public records, transferring ownership to himself or someone else, typically a willing accomplice. The accomplice may be using a stolen identity.
2. If the property has a mortgage against it, the con artist will generally also falsify a mortgage satisfaction, as discussed in the following section, to fool lenders into thinking that the previous mortgage was paid in full.
3. The con artist either takes out a loan against the property or quickly sells it to cash out on the deal. (Fraudsters occasionally take title and then lease the property, but this is a high-risk,

slow-return approach that rarely pays off. Property thefts are almost always discovered.)

The original homeowner can regain possession of the property because, in most cases, a forged deed is void and does not legally transfer ownership. If the con artist sold the property, the buyer, who probably purchased title insurance, is reimbursed by the title company. If a lender funded a loan for purchase of the property, the lender purchased title insurance and would be reimbursed by their title company as well. As you can see, the big losers in these scams are usually the title companies who must reimburse the victims.

Certain states are more vulnerable to these phony deed scams because they make it easy to record forged documents. In Michigan, for example, deeds formerly required two witnesses to the person's signature, one of which could be a notary. Today you don't even need a witness, just a notary, which makes the process of recording forged deeds much easier.

Mortgage Satisfactions

When homeowners apply for a refinance mortgage, the lender searches the title to make sure it has no other liens against it. Any existing liens need to be paid off before closing. In phony deed scams, the con artist often applies for a loan against the property, so she needs to make it look as though the property is free and clear of any other liens. To accomplish this feat, the con artist simply creates and files a false mortgage satisfaction or reconveyance, making it appear, on paper, that the existing loan has been paid in full. At closing, the proceeds go directly to the con artist rather than being used to pay off the prior lender.

Sometimes, phony mortgage satisfactions are used as a means of perpetrating a large, complicated fraud scheme. Other times, property owners use them to scam lenders out of money when they're facing hard times or simply to use a property as a cash cow to dupe multiple lenders into approving several loans for the same property.

CASE STUDY

One of the most brazen con artist duos, Matthew B. Cox and Rebecca M. Hauck, used forged deeds and mortgage satisfactions to defraud homeowners and lenders out of more than $1 million. Jeff Testerman of the *St. Petersburg Times* penned several articles about this couple, dubbed the Bonnie and Clyde of mortgage fraud.

In one scam, Cox allegedly used a stolen identity to rent a home owned by Theresa A. Knight. Hauck obtained a counterfeit driver's license in Knight's name and then headed to a local UPS store outside Atlanta and purchased a mail drop box at the store in Knight's name.

Cox then allegedly filed a phony satisfaction of mortgage document at the Leon County Clerk of Courts, making it appear as though the homeowner, Knight, had paid off the mortgage on her home in full. Hauck then applied for a new mortgage on the property for $53,000, using her fake I.D. and other information she had obtained about Knight. Hauck listed the mail drop box as her address.

At the closing for the loan, Hauck signed the documents "T. Knight," and the loan proceeds were deposited into separate accounts that Cox had allegedly set up using stolen identities.

Cox and Hauck repeated their formula for success across several southern states, according to their federal indictments, including Florida, Georgia, and South Carolina, leaving a trail of victims who faced foreclosure and ruined credit.

CASE STUDY

In Greenwich, Connecticut, real estate developer Andrew Kissel allegedly became a master of using fake mortgage satisfactions to con lenders out of more than $20 million. The facts outlined in his indictment allege the following:

- On July 26, 2004, Kissel obtained a mortgage for $1,620,800 to buy a 2.4 acre property at 43 Burning Tree Road.

Spotting the **S**igns

Unfortunately, due to the nature of phony deed scams, you have no early warning signs to nip the scam in the bud. However, the earlier you act, the better are your chances of retaining your home and controlling the damage. Watch for the following red flags:

- A bank calls to inform you that you've missed one or more payments on a mortgage loan you never applied for.

- You receive a foreclosure notice from a lending institution you never borrowed money from.

- And, of course, you may be caught up in a tax deed scam if someone shows up at your home with a tax deed or tax lien certificate claiming to be the new owner of your home and instructing you to vacate the premises or sign a paper deeding the home over to them.

- On or around February 2, 2005, Kissel filed a mortgage satisfaction with the town clerk, falsely showing that the first mortgage had been paid in full.
- On March 22, 2005, Kissel closed on a construction loan for $4,500,000, the proceeds of which were to be used to build a new home on the property. The lender approved this second loan completely unaware that the first loan had never been paid off.
- As of July 7, 2005, Kissel had drawn approximately $1.5 million from the second loan.
- On or around April 9, 2005, Kissel filed another mortgage satisfaction indicating that the lien on the second loan had been released, even though he had not paid off the second loan.
- In May 2005, Kissel took out a third loan against the same property for $1 million.
- Shortly after taking out the third loan, Kissel took out a fourth loan (a construction loan) for $4,525,000. Because the

$1 million loan had not been recorded yet, it didn't show up as a lien against the property, and he was able to close on the fourth loan. When the lender went to record the mortgage on the fourth loan, the lender discovered the existence of the third loan. Kissel claimed that the third lender had attached the mortgage to the wrong property. He then proceeded to file a fake mortgage satisfaction for the third loan, ensuring that the fourth loan would be approved.

Prior to pleading guilty to federal fraud charges, Kissel was found stabbed to death in his apartment.

CASE STUDY

A retired couple had the misfortune of meeting up with a savvy con artist who came very close to stealing their home of 30 years right out from under them, and may eventually succeed and get away with it.

The couple owned their home free and clear but had fallen on hard times and were unable to pay $10,000 they owed in back taxes. They called a loan officer who told them that the loan amount was too small to appeal to any lenders. He referred them to a friend who specialized in similar cases.

The loan officer's friend showed up, befriended the couple, paid the $10,000 in taxes, and set up a payment plan. They thought that they were signing papers to process the loan—just some blank paperwork that their newfound friend would complete later. It turned out that the documents they had signed included a quitclaim deed, transferring ownership of the property to the con artist.

Later, he took out a mortgage on the property for $135,000 and didn't make the payments. The couple received notice that they were in foreclosure. The bank bought the property at auction and initiated proceedings to have the couple evicted. Fortunately for them, they

Protect Yourself

Tax deeds, fake deeds, and fraudulent mortgage satisfactions are fairly easy ways to rip off homeowners and lenders. To protect yourself against the con artists who use these tactics, take the following preventive measures:

- Don't leave a property vacant for any length of time. Vacant homes are particularly vulnerable to phony deed scams. If a family member is going to be out of the house for an extended period, check on the house, keep it properly maintained, and check the mail. Ask neighbors to inform you of any suspicious activities, such as the home going up for sale.

- Pay your property taxes and pay heed to any notices of late payments. By paying your property taxes on time, you know that nobody could have possibly purchased a tax deed or tax lien certificate for your home.

- Don't sign a deed just because someone claims that you're obligated to do so.

- Read documents carefully before signing them.

- Don't sign any documents that have blanks that can be filled in later to your detriment.

- Know your rights. When someone shows up at your house claiming to be the new owner because they purchased a tax deed or tax lien certificate, do some research to determine whether what they're claiming is true. Check out *www.professorprofits.com/states/index. php* for the tax sale rules in your state. (This is not a recommendation or representation as to the validity of any of the products or programs sold through the site.)

- Contact an attorney when you first suspect that something is amiss. A con artist's success often hinges on homeowner ignorance. A real estate attorney can help protect your rights. In many cases, simply informing you of your rights is sufficient.

had a very proactive daughter who began to tell everyone, and one of those everyones was a real estate agent who attended a seminar on real estate and mortgage fraud.

The agent referred the couple to the real estate and mortgage fraud specialist who conducted the seminar, and the couple hired an attorney to represent them. The attorney processed a stay of eviction so the couple could remain in the house while the judge examined the evidence. During the writing of this book, the judge was still in the process of reviewing the facts of the case, and law enforcement officials were considering the possibility of filing criminal charges against the con artist.

15

FORECLOSURE SCAMS:

Fleecing Distressed Homeowners

Distressed homeowners facing foreclosure are easy prey for con artists and greedy opportunists. Embarrassed, angry, and often desperate, they're willing to believe anyone who comes along offering a compassionate ear and a simple solution that enables them to remain in their home and perhaps even erase their debt. Charismatic, smooth-talking con artists often target these vulnerable homeowners and befriend them only to rip them off.

In this chapter, you will probe the depths of human depravation as we reveal the slimy underbellies of foreclosure con artists and uncover the tricks they use to lure trusting homeowners into their traps. We relate two real-world case studies showing foreclosure rescue scams at work, uncover the warning signs to watch out for, and show you how to protect yourself and your home against these wily shysters.

THE MANY FACES OF FORECLOSURE SCAMS

Foreclosure scams assume many forms, ranging from brazen stealing to more subtle deceptions designed to strip the homeowner's equity from the property. They may even involve scams designed by homeowners to sidestep a legal foreclosure. In the following sections, we describe the most common types of foreclosure fraud, but keep in mind that con artists are constantly inventing new variations on the theme.

Foreclosure Rescue and Equity Stripping

Foreclosure rescue is any program that induces homeowners to part with the title to their home based on claims that doing so will save the home from foreclosure. While not always illegal in and of themselves, these programs are usually misleading, often fraudulent, and sometimes criminal. Following are some of the strategies employed by foreclosure rescue con artists:

- A loan shark may attempt to convince the homeowners to refinance their way out of a financial setback by taking out a foreclosure *bailout loan*—a typically high-interest loan for an amount sufficient to reinstate the loan. The operator knows that the homeowner probably won't be able to make the payments, in which case the loan shark will foreclose on the bailout loan when the owners go into default and take possession of the home.
- An "investor" may convince homeowners who have a substantial amount of equity built up in their property to sell the property to them for significantly less than the property is worth, with the promise that the homeowners can live there as long as they want. As soon as the homeowners sign the papers, the con artist evicts them.
- The con artist promises the homeowners that she will take care of everything. All they have to do is sign the home over

to the con artist using a quitclaim deed. Usually, the con artist will offer to lease the home back to the homeowners for a
year at a rent higher than the amount of the mortgage with
an option to purchase at the end of the lease term. Although
the con artist promises to assist the homeowners in cleaning
up their credit during the year lease term, this is not done
and the homeowners are seldom able to exercise the option.
The con artist records the deed and becomes the legal owner
of the property. When the homeowners are unable to obtain
financing to exercise their purchase option at the end of the
lease period, the con artist evicts the homeowners.

- The con artist agrees to assist the homeowners by helping to
repair their credit and structure a repayment plan with the
mortgage company. As part of this service, the con artist has
the homeowners sign a power of attorney in the name of the
con artist and give the con artist money each month to pay
the homeowners' mortgage and other bills. The con artist files
for change of address on behalf of the homeowners with the
homeowners' creditors, so that the homeowners will no longer
receive late notices. The con artist doesn't make any of the
homeowners' payments and just absconds with the money. The
lender forecloses and the homeowners lose the house.

In the classic foreclosure rescue scam, the operator obtains foreclosure information from the county register of deeds or county clerk
and then approaches the homeowners in person or by telephone,
often within days of the scheduled foreclosure sale. The operator
offers the homeowners the opportunity to save their home by entering into a lease option contract—the homeowners can sell the property to the operator or another party and then lease it for a year or
more with the option to buy it back at the end of that time.

The operator usually offers to assist the homeowners in rebuild-
ing their credit during the lease so they can qualify for a loan when
the lease expires and then buy back the property. The offer of assistance comes with no money-back guarantee, and the operator rare-

Legitimate Foreclosure Assistance

Not all foreclosure rescue programs are scams. Some programs provide credit counseling and assistance to borrowers who experience financial setbacks. If you find yourself facing foreclosure, contact a HUD-approved housing counseling agency listed in the Foreclosure section of HUD's website at *www.hud.gov*.

provides any real assistance. When the lease period expires, the homeowners can't qualify for a loan and end up forfeiting their option to repurchase their home. The operator then evicts the homeowners and takes possession of the property. In some cases, the operator immediately refinances the property as soon as the title is transferred to his name, stripping any equity that the homeowners had in the property. The fraudster may simply strip the equity and move on, quitclaiming his interest in the property back to the homeowners and leaving them with two mortgages to pay. Now, if the homeowners want to save their house, they must come up with enough cash to pay off the first and second mortgage along with any foreclosure rescue "fees" they paid to the operator.

Some real estate investment seminars go so far as to promote and teach this "investment strategy" and it is one of the most often taught ways of buying property with "no money down." We've never seen a seminar advertising that it will teach investors how to earn a reasonable rate of interest by helping people. The sole purpose of the strategy is not to assist homeowners or "rescue" them from foreclosure, but to obtain property and strip the equity from it or simply take it from the homeowners.

Foreclosure rescue scams always increase when the housing market begins to decline. In early 2005, the number of these operations increased exponentially, and as foreclosure rates continue to rise, we see an inordinate increase in the incidence and frequency of such schemes. In hard-hit areas, including California and Illinois, states

have passed statutes to protect consumers. The vast majority of legal actions taken in foreclosure rescue schemes are instituted by state attorneys general under Unfair Business Practice statutes.

Recovering the Excess Proceeds from a Foreclosure Sale

When a lender forecloses on a property, it's usually auctioned off to the highest bidder. The money that the high bidder pays for the property is paid to the lien holders in a preestablished order of priority—typically based on the date on which the loan obligation was recorded. Generally, the property taxes are paid off first, followed by the first lien (first mortgage), followed by junior liens (other loans), judgments, and other tax liens.

If any money remains after all of these liens are paid off, the foreclosed upon homeowners are usually entitled to collect the excess proceeds. In some states, the excess is automatically paid to the homeowners after all other lien holders are paid. In other states, the homeowners must file a claim (usually with the county or the local court) to obtain the proceeds. In any event, obtaining the proceeds is a routine and very simple process.

If the homeowner had plenty of equity built up in the property, the excess proceeds could be fairly substantial, and that's where the con artist steps in. He tries to scam these already financially strapped homeowners out of part or all of the money that rightfully belongs to them. The con artist typically approaches the homeowners shortly after the sale and employs one of the following methods to get his hands on the money:

- The con artist describes the process of claiming the money as very complicated and offers to help the homeowners in exchange for some exorbitant fee or a percentage of the proceeds.
- The con artist offers to "buy" the homeowners' rights to the proceeds for pennies on the dollar, convincing them that the

proceeds are much less than they really are, and the process is much more complicated and time-consuming than it really is.

- Sometimes the con artist avoids approaching the homeowners and just petitions the court for release of the funds without the homeowners' knowledge or permission.

Foreclosure Bailouts

Foreclosure bailouts are generally masterminded by homeowners facing foreclosure. With insufficient income and bad credit, the homeowners can't qualify for a new loan to refinance their way out of foreclosure, so they have a friend or relative take out a new loan to pretend-buy the property. The homeowners then make the payments on the new loan.

In essence, a foreclosure bailout consists of using a straw borrower to obtain the loan. The straw borrower who applies for and obtains the loan has committed fraud and, unless the homeowners have resolved the issue that pushed them into foreclosure in the first place, they're unlikely to be able to make payments on the new loan. The homeowner will just end up in foreclosure again, ruining the credit of the friend or relative who went along with the scheme. The likelihood that they will be able to keep up on the payments is low because the new mortgage is usually higher than the old mortgage. This is due to the fact that the past-due payment amount on the prior mortgage was likely added to the principal balance when the new loan was obtained.

CASE STUDY

Joe Johnson and his wife Helen were in their 70s. They had worked their entire lives and had saved their money. They had a successful business, which they sold, and they purchased a nice home in a retirement community. The payments they received from their business sale more than covered their mortgage.

Spotting the **S**igns

Foreclosure scams occur in any area but are more prevalent in cities and states with high foreclosure rates. If you've received a notice of default or foreclosure, realize that these are public documents that con artists use to target potential victims, and the notice makes you a high-profile mark. The notice should make you more vigilant about the following warning signs:

- Anyone who tells you that you have only one or two options to stop foreclosure. You usually have more than a half-dozen options.

- A company or individual offers to help you save your home from foreclosure if you deed the house over to them

- Anyone who tells you *not* to contact your lender or some other professional for assistance

- Someone who claims to be able to eliminate your mortgage. See chapter 16 for details on mortgage elimination scams.

- Anyone who offers to loan you the money to pay off the foreclosing lender at a high rate of interest. If you can't make your current payments, how are you going to make the payments on this loan?

- An "investor" who offers to buy your house for significantly less than market value, especially if you have a lot of equity built up in it. You may have other, better options.

- Anyone who offers to help you collect the excess proceeds from a foreclosure sale. You can collect the proceeds yourself—it's not difficult.

The new owners of Joe and Helen's business were not successful, and the business declared bankruptcy, cutting off the monthly payments the Johnsons had relied on to make their mortgage payments. After the Johnsons missed several payments, the bank recorded a notice of default, and the Johnsons were facing foreclosure.

The Johnsons were considering selling the property and downsizing to save their considerable investment when they were approached by their "guardian angel," Mr. Meyes. Meyes, who attended the same church as the Johnsons, owned a real estate brokerage and an escrow company. He sympathized with them and said he wanted to help. After running a credit check and determining they could not refinance due to credit problems, Meyes offered them another way out.

Meyes told the Johnsons that he would find an "investor" who would come on title with them and would loan them one year's worth of payments on their mortgage by paying the money to their mortgage company directly. During the next year, Meyes would help them repair their credit, and, within the year, they would be able to refinance at a lower rate, and the investor would be removed from the title. The investor would be paid $10,000 for this service. Feeling they had no other option to save their home, the Johnsons agreed to this scenario and signed a deed putting the investor on title.

Six months later, the Johnsons received an eviction notice from the investor who claimed that the home belonged to him. The Johnsons learned that a deed had been recorded that transferred the title to the investor and that they were no longer the owners of record. They also found out that the investor had taken out a loan against their home for its full appreciated value—taking almost $500,000 of equity from their home!

CASE STUDY

In Michigan, two brothers acting as investors achieved substantial financial success by using lease option contracts to prey on distressed homeowners. The brothers would meet with homeowners who were facing foreclosure, lend a sympathetic ear, and offer to help them out. They convinced the homeowners to deed the property over to them and buy it back under a lease option contract. The brothers led the homeowners to believe that they would pay off the underlying mortgage—something the brothers didn't actually do.

If the homeowners had any equity built up in the house, the brothers would refinance and strip all the equity out of it. If the homeowners had no equity in the house, the brothers would simply

Protect Yourself

The key to protecting yourself against foreclosure fraud is to seek assistance as soon as possible from well-established institutions and programs that have a proven track record rather than from a complete stranger who comes knocking, calling, or mailing you letters with offers to "help." Taking the right steps is the best way to avoid taking the wrong steps. One of the best first places to go for assistances is a HUD-approved credit counselor. You can find a list of these in the Foreclosure section on HUD's website at *www.hud.gov*.

Foreclosure is the result of payment stress, which is either temporary or permanent. *Temporary payment stress* is typically brought on by a one-time event, such as illness, job loss, or unexpected expenses. It causes a borrower to miss a few mortgage payments but does not impact the borrower's ability to make payments on a permanent basis. *Permanent payment stress* is a chronic problem, which can be the result of a serious medical condition that's expensive to treat, a substance abuse or gambling problem, divorce, the death of a breadwinner, uncontrolled spending, or having an adjustable-rate mortgage with an interest rate that suddenly increases to a point at which you can't afford the payments.

The right steps vary according to the type of payment stress you're experiencing—temporary or permanent.

collect the payments until the lender foreclosed on the house and evicted the homeowners. How is this possible? In Michigan, once the property is auctioned off at the sheriff sale, the lender has no reason to contact the homeowners and let them know about the impending eviction. The homeowners have six months prior to being evicted to redeem the property by paying off the loan balance and any late fees and penalties. But the homeowners were convinced that the brothers were taking care of everything and that their guardian angels (the brothers) had paid off the mortgage. They believed that the reason they weren't hearing from the lender was that the matter had been resolved.

Thinking that everything had been taken care of, the homeowners continued to make their monthly payments to the brothers, completely unaware that when the redemption period expired in six months, the lender was going to have them evicted.

One way Michigan could shut down this type of fraud would be to require the lender to send notices to the homeowners during the redemption period so they would be aware that the lender was not paid off and that the eviction was proceeding as scheduled.

Temporary Payment Stress

When you experience a temporary financial setback, consider the following options:

- Always contact the lender immediately. The lender can restructure the repayment of missed payments or tack on the missed payments to the end of the loan. These are referred to as Loan Workouts or Loan Modifications.
- Obtain credit counseling from a reputable credit counselor. Consolidating your debt with a single loan may result in a monthly payment that's less than the total monthly payments on all of your other loans.
- Refinance. If you have sufficient equity in the property, you may be able to take out a new mortgage and pay off the old mortgage.

Permanent Payment Stress

Permanent payment stress is a more serious issue and often has an underlying problem that must be resolved or at least acknowledged. Consider the following options:

- Address or acknowledge the underlying problem. Can it be resolved?
- Contact your lender immediately to learn your options.
- If the underlying problem can't be resolved, or you have no realistic option to save your home, consider selling it and finding

more affordable accommodations. Selling the home gives you the greatest chance of recovering any equity you have built up, and the sooner you place the house on the market, the better. Once the foreclosure is public knowledge, you're less likely to receive offers for the fair market value of the property.

- If you have little or no equity in the property or the balance of the loan exceeds the property value, the lender may agree to a *short sale*—accepting a partial payoff of the loan or a *deed in lieu*—where the homeowners sign over the deed to the property instead of forcing the lender to foreclose.

Institutional lenders are not interested in foreclosing on a borrower's home, regardless of the equity in the home. Lenders generally lose money in foreclosure situations and even in situations where there is substantial equity, they will seldom make a profit. The notion that lenders want to foreclose to steal your home is an urban myth. At most foreclosure sales, the lender is allowed to bid an amount only equivalent to recover the balance of the loan plus accrued interest and the cost of foreclosure. If the property has significant equity, a third party typically purchases the home and the lender is paid the amount owed on the loan. Any additional money paid by the third-party purchaser goes first to pay off other liens with the balance paid back to the homeowners.

When the homeowners have little or no equity in the property or the debt is close to or exceeds the property value, the lender cannot even recover the amount owed. Lenders are motivated to work with borrowers to structure payment plans or modify loan terms in order to keep the borrower in the property. Work with your lender and with reputable known agencies if facing foreclosure. Don't trust the people who knock on your door before the day of the sale!

16

MORTGAGE ELIMINATION SCHEMES

Banks, mortgage companies, and other lenders offer plenty of legitimate ways to eliminate a mortgage. You can pay off the mortgage, borrow less, refinance for a shorter-term loan at a lower interest rate, make payments every two weeks rather than every month, pay a little extra each month toward the principal, or sell the property.

Now, there's an even better way. Dozens of companies promise to help homeowners completely eliminate their 30-year mortgages in a matter of months for a flat fee of only a few thousand dollars up front! What a deal! For 3000 bucks or so, all you have to do is kick back in your lounge chair and twiddle your thumbs, and in less than a year, you can own your home free and clear! Even better, you may qualify to cash out tens of thousands of dollars in equity!

In this chapter, we reveal how these mortgage elimination schemes work and why they're so attractive—and so illegal. We shed some light on the red flags you need to watch out for and then tell you exactly what to do to steer clear of these scams. We also provide a case study that demonstrates just how devastating an actual mortgage elimination scheme can be.

BEHIND THE SCENES WITH MORTGAGE ELIMINATION SCHEMES

Mortgage elimination or *debt elimination* schemes twist logic in such a way as to convince people that the strategy is a perfectly legitimate way to wash away all debt and even earn a profit of tens of thousands of dollars. Let's examine how one of these schemes unfolds.

First, the mortgage eliminators (a.k.a. con artists) post ads on websites, in Internet pop-ups, in classifieds, and wherever else they can advertise their mortgage elimination techniques. These are usually pitched as "What the government doesn't want you to know" or "What the banks don't want you to know." Sometimes this is advertised as *debt elimination,* because the scheme can purportedly also erase the balance on car loans, credit cards, and other debts.

The next step is to sell the theory that mortgage elimination is perfectly legal and it works. This is the fun part. Con artists have concocted all sorts of creative arguments to prove the legitimacy of mortgage elimination. According to one argument, banks don't really loan *their* money. They loan money they have borrowed, and if you trace that money back to its source, it is money that the government printed, so it has no real value—it's just paper and ink. As the borrower, *you actually generated the money,* because a promissory note is an asset, and when you signed the note, you gave the bank an asset and they gave you nothing. In essence, the bank made money off of your signature, so the mortgage note is meaningless, and you don't owe the money. In fact, the bank owes *you* money!

The con artists toss a few extras into the argument to make it sound more convincing, often quoting politicians and Federal Reserve documents out of context to prove their point. They are also careful to mention that banks, mortgage companies, and the FBI will tell you that mortgage elimination is a scam, not because it is illegal, but because the establishment is so afraid that if more people knew the truth, the big bad banks would no longer be able to cheat people out of their money.

The underlying arguments and promises vary. Some con artists claim that humanitarian aid is available to pay off mortgages. Others build complex pyramid schemes in which participants pay off the mortgages of other participants. And some offer to review your mortgage documents for technical or legal violations that will force lenders to forgive part or all of the mortgage balance.

Assuming you buy into whatever argument the con artist presents, you send three or four or five thousand dollars to the mortgage eliminator who promises to guide you through the process, file the necessary paperwork, and attend to the complex legalities of the deal. With some con artists, that's the end of it. They pocket the money they receive up front, and then you never hear from them again.

Other mortgage eliminators who are more ambitious take the scam even further. They may sign a mortgage satisfaction or reconveyance as if they were authorized to do so by the lender, and record it with the county clerk or recorder. The mortgage remains in place and the homeowners still owe the money to the bank, but when the county clerk records the mortgage discharge, the records make it appear as though the homeowners own the property free and clear.

Now that the homeowners appear to own the home free and clear, the homeowners apply for one or more additional loans on the property—with the generous assistance of the mortgage eliminator, of course. When the loan or loans are approved, the mortgage eliminator and the homeowners split the proceeds, often with the mortgage eliminator walking away with the lion's share of the cash.

As far as the homeowners can see, they have a new mortgage with similar monthly payments, but they now have $50,000 to $100,000 cash in the bank. What they fail to realize, and what the mortgage eliminator fails to mention, is that the first mortgage was never really discharged by the bank; it was discharged only according to a fraudulent document recorded in the county clerk's office.

Spotting the Signs

Mortgage elimination schemes are not new. Lenders have file cabinets full of cases in which people have tried various debt elimination strategies. These schemes sound new only to the homeowners who fall for them and lose their money or their homes or both. We know of only one way to eliminate debt—pay it off. When you come across an ad for mortgage or debt elimination, skim the ad for the following red flags:

- Any claim that you can eliminate debt without paying it off

- An argument that U.S. currency is not valid because the United States no longer observes the gold standard—it's just paper money that the government prints

- Claims that mortgages and other loans are invalid because the mortgages are based on a "lack of consideration." In other words, the lender provided you with nothing of value.

- Promises that others—agencies, not-for-profit organizations, or participants in the program—will pay off your mortgage or other debt for you. Nobody other than you will pay off your mortgage.

- A deal that just seems too good to be true. It probably is.

Eventually, the bank that made the original loan, or the banks that made the subsequent loans, spot the scam and confront the homeowners. By this time, the mortgage eliminator is long gone, leaving the homeowners with one or more unpaid mortgages, a legal morass, pending foreclosure proceedings, and possible criminal charges.

CASE STUDY

One of the most publicized mortgage elimination schemes was orchestrated by the Dorean Group, a business set up by Scott Heineman and Kurt Johnson in 2004. Dorean offered a program whereby the company would "eliminate" a mortgage for a flat fee ranging from $2,000 to $3,500.

On the homeowners' behalf, Dorean would send a package to the lender asserting its theories and claiming that the lender must respond within ten days. If the lender did not respond, the lender supposedly provided "consent by silence" to the appointment of Heineman and Johnson as power of attorney to reconvey the trust deed/record satisfactions.

Initially, homeowners who enrolled in the program praised Dorean online and claimed they had proof that their mortgages were eliminated. They did have this proof in the form of recorded documents of satisfaction—documents showing that their mortgages had been paid in full. Heineman and Johnson had signed these under the "power of attorney" they claimed was created by the lender's failure to properly respond.

Unfortunately for the homeowners, these documents were not valid and did not actually affect the mortgage at all. The homeowners could have just as easily kept the $3,000 and signed and recorded the phony satisfactions themselves.

The program was based on a couple of flawed arguments. The first argument was that the lenders didn't actually provide anything of value to the borrowers. According to the argument, the wire transfer of funds used "vapor money"—in other words, the money wasn't real; it didn't exist. The argument is flawed because it fails to account for the fact that the sellers actually were paid and a real property was transferred to the new owner (the person who was now trying to claim that he received nothing of value through the loan).

Another argument was that the promissory note that the borrowers signed when taking on the mortgage was actually a valuable asset that the borrowers gave to the lender. According to Dorean's two arguments, then, the borrowers provided something of value to the lender, but the lender provided nothing of value (only vapor money) to the borrowers, so the lender actually owed the borrowers something of value—not the other way around. This argument, of course, fails to consider that a promissory note is valuable only so long as the borrowers honor the promise to pay. Otherwise, a promissory note could be considered "vapor money" as well. In other words,

Protect **Y**ourself

Fortunately, mortgage elimination schemes are not subtle; the perpetrator tells you exactly what he's going to do—eliminate your mortgage so you'll never have to make another monthly mortgage payment for the rest of your life. When you hear that, start running as fast as you can in the opposite direction. Don't pay money to anyone who claims to be able to eliminate your mortgage. If you're tempted to participate, wait a couple of years to see whether the perpetrators are indicted and homeowners lose their life savings. Any legitimate system for eliminating mortgages will bear the test of time, and with a 30-year mortgage, you have plenty of time to take advantage of the wonderful offer.

the borrowers have provided nothing of value until the borrowers pay off the mortgage.

Heineman and Johnson were indicted by the federal government. The last we heard was that they are currently in custody and awaiting trial on numerous charges including conspiracy to commit bank fraud, mail fraud, and wire fraud. An indictment is just an allegation by the government, and all defendants are presumed innocent until they are convicted. Johnson has already done jail time as he was previously convicted of securities fraud.

Many homeowners who followed Dorean's advice stopped making their monthly mortgage payments and ended up losing their homes. They believed that they could get something for nothing. A little common sense could have saved them.

Unfortunately, Dorean wasn't the first proponent of mortgage elimination to be peddling this nonsense to homeowners, and it certainly won't be the last. Visit *www.mortgagefraudblog.com* to read about other similar scams, including one perpetrated by Redwood Trust and another by Brixdale.

17

LYING FOR DOLLARS II:

Borrowing Money Out of Thin Air

Air loans are the ultimate con. The con artist erects an imaginary world of her very own, consisting of fictional borrowers (or stolen identities), employers, appraisers, credit agencies, and anything else she needs to secure a loan. None of this exists—at least legitimately—but the fiction more often than not convinces lenders to hand loads of cash over to the con artist.

This chapter explains air loans and presents a compelling case study demonstrating how an air loan artist plies his craft. Although air loans may not directly victimize homeowners, these scams often rely on some form of identity theft, so we reveal the warning signs that consumers need to look out for and precautions you can take to protect your personal information from getting into the wrong hands.

WHAT IS AN AIR LOAN?

An air loan is a mortgage that's been approved based on qualifying information that's false from A to Z. What type of qualifying information are we talking about? Everything that shows up on the loan application and is included in the closing packet is subject to fabrication, including the following:

- *Homeowner/Borrower/Buyer.* The homeowner, borrower, or buyer who is applying for the loan is usually a fictional person (with a fictional identity and credit history) or a real person whose identity has been stolen. Sometimes the con artist uses the identity of a deceased person or takes advantage of recent immigrants.
- *Collateral.* Collateral used to secure the loan is typically worthless and sometimes even nonexistent. The property may consist of a gutted shell of a home or a vacant lot, or the con artist lists the address of a property that doesn't exist.
- *Appraisal.* The appraisal is often a complete fabrication. The appraiser doesn't exist, or the appraiser's identity has been stolen, and the appraisal is forged.
- *Broker.* The person originating the loan is usually a fictional character or a real broker who's completely unaware that her identity has been stolen and used to provide false verification of the loan documents. Sometimes, the broker is in on the scheme.
- *Escrow company.* The escrow company handling the closing may not exist. Sometimes, the fraudsters use the name of a real escrow company or create their own title company and simply provide a phony address or have the cash proceeds wired to their own account or to multiple accounts to avoid detection.
- *Pay stubs.* Fake pay stubs and W-2's are often used to verify employment and income.
- *Bank statements.* Phony bank statements show that the borrowers have sufficient funds in their savings and checking accounts to obtain loan approval. Asset rentals may also be used to prove that the applicant owns valuable collateral.
- *Title commitment.* Counterfeit title commitments verify that the property exists and is free and clear of any liens and encumbrances.

- *Closing statements.* Fabricated and forged closing statements make it appear as though all parties involved in the transaction are completely aware of all the details. The only party who's not aware of what's going on is usually the lender, who often has no representation at the closing table.

In an air loan, the challenge is to find a single thread of truth or a single real person who's involved in the transaction. Often the only way to find the ringleaders is to follow the money trail—a trail that typically disappears at the coastline and vanishes into one or more offshore accounts.

"The worst of the air loans are the ones involving identity theft," says Ann Fulmer, cofounder of GREFPAC (Georgia Real Estate Fraud Prevention and Awareness Coalition) and vice president of Interthinx, a leading provider of fraud prevention products to the mortgage industry. "With those loans, the bank is robbed, the community's damaged, and a person who's built a good credit rating is suddenly on the brink of financial disaster. It's a tremendous ordeal to restore your credit after your identity's been stolen. And it's especially infuriating because your only 'crime' was working hard to pay your bills."

HOW DOES IDENTITY THEFT FACTOR IN?

Perpetrators of air loan scams aren't about to use their own names and information to apply for loans. They need to either create a fictional loan applicant or steal someone's identity. In most cases, stealing the identity of an actual person is most effective because it saves the con artist the trouble of coming up with a phony name, Social Security number, and driver's license. After all, an invalid Social Security number could draw some suspicion.

Con artists have devised a host of sinister schemes to steal identities ranging from high-tech computer hacks into financial institutions to low-tech methods, such as stealing mail and rummaging through

The Growing Problem of Stolen Professional Identities

Lenders in the mortgage industry are currently facing a growing problem of professional identity theft—fraudsters stealing the identities (names and license numbers) of real estate professionals, including appraisers, attorneys, accountants, mortgage brokers, and real estate agents. They then use these stolen identities to originate fraudulent loans. Professional identity theft is a serious problem because the lender ends up dealing with documents that have essentially been manufactured out of thin air yet have the air of authenticity.

Lenders rely on local real estate professionals to provide valid and verified data on the value of the collateral, income of the borrower, compliance with closing procedures, and so on. When these items are utterly false, but are authenticated with the identities of real professionals, the lenders' underwriting decisions are likewise flawed, and lenders end up making loans that they otherwise would not have approved.

For real estate professionals, identity theft can be devastating because they often face legal claims, complaints against their licenses, and lawsuits from the lenders and borrowers who are injured by the false documents. Stealing the identities of real estate professionals and then using them to commit crimes ruins their reputations and typically results in their loss of time, money, and future business opportunities.

The perpetrators of these crimes are usually very sophisticated and knowledgeable. They're often real estate professionals themselves who use their insider information to steal their colleagues' identities and fabricate the necessary paperwork.

garbage cans. The Federal Trade Commission (FTC) lists the following five most common methods for stealing identities:

- *Dumpster diving.* Thieves rummage through trash looking for bills or other paper with your personal information on it.
- *Skimming.* A crooked server at a restaurant or a store clerk takes your credit card and scans it into a portable credit card reader when you're not looking.
- *Phishing.* The con artist dupes you into handing over your credit card information by posing as a legitimate financial

institution or business. Phishing is a common method used on the Internet. The con artist will send you a phony email message, display a pop-up message on your computer, or set up an official looking website to gather your data.

- *Changing your address.* The fraudster fills out a change of address form for your mailing address and has all of your mail, including billing statements and credit card applications, forwarded to him.

- *Old-fashioned stealing.* Identity thieves often steal wallets and purses, mail, including bank and credit card statements, preapproved credit offers, and new checks or tax information. They steal personnel records from their employers or bribe employees who have access to the information to steal it for them.

CASE STUDY

Gerald P. Small III was no small-time air loan con artist. According to court reports, using two separate schemes, he and his crew managed to obtain over $255 million in fraudulent loans from various U.S. financial institutions and ruin the credit histories of the many people from whom they stole identities. Small's first scheme, which he pulled off with associate Robert Bichon, was a classic chunking scheme. (You can find out more about chunking schemes in chapter 10.)

According to court documents, the second scheme began in February 2003. Small started a company called Amerifunding in his wife's name and then obtained a multimillion-dollar warehouse line of credit from Flagstar (the lender). Through his personal guarantees and false financial statements, Small convinced Flagstar to approve several increases to his line of credit. He also obtained a separate line of credit from another company, IMPAC Warehouse Lending Group, by supplying similar phony financial statements.

Another of Small's conspirators, Chad Heinrich, used the proceeds of the fraudulent loan from Flagstar to purchase Twentieth Century Mortgage, Inc. Heinrich then proceeded to obtain a $25 mil-

Spotting the Signs

By nature, an air loan has few red flags that would draw any attention or scrutiny. After all, if air loans were easy to spot, no lender would ever consider approving such loans. However, because air loans often employ some sort of identity theft, consumers need to be able to spot the following warning signs of identity theft:

- You stop receiving mail.
- You receive an email notice with a link to a website requesting that you enter login information or other sensitive information.
- A representative of a company you've done business with or have never heard of calls you out of the blue and starts asking questions.
- A bill collector calls to inform you of overdue debts on accounts you never opened or for products or services you never ordered or received.
- You are denied a loan because of some outstanding issue in your credit history that you were completely unaware of.
- You receive a notice in the mail about a house you never purchased, a job you never held, or an apartment you never rented.
- You receive a "welcome call" from a mortgage lender regarding a house you don't recall buying.

lion line of credit from Flagstar using phony financial statements similar to the ones initially used by Small. Small then directed Heinrich, Charles Winnett, and other employees to continue to submit loan applications to Flagstar and IMPAC on behalf of Amerifunding and Twentieth Century Mortgage. These loan applications were packed with false information. In many cases, the loan applicants' names and information were stolen or made up, and the borrowers had no intention of purchasing the properties listed on the applications.

To collect the proceeds from the loans, Small had employees set up several shell corporations: TDF Mortgage Funding, Inc., Security

Protect **Y**ourself

The big losers in air loan schemes are the lenders who actually hand over the cash to the con artists, but average citizens suffer as well when their identities are stolen and used to perpetrate these scams. You can protect yourself from identity theft by guarding your personal information and acting quickly when you notice that your personal information is being used without your authorization. Some steps to take to protect yourself include the following:

- Guard your personal information. Don't supply information over the phone, via mail, or on the Internet unless you've initiated contact and trust the company you're dealing with.

- Don't leave mail out in your mail box for the mail carrier to pick up. Deposit it in a post office collection box or drop it off at your local post office.

- Don't leave delivered mail sitting in your mailbox for any length of time.

- If you go on vacation, have the post office hold your mail.

- If you move, complete a change of address form at the post office to have mail forwarded to your new address starting on your moving date.

- Carry fewer credit cards and identifying information in your wallet or purse.

- Don't carry around your Social Security card. Memorize your number and store your card in a safe, secure place.

- Give out your Social Security number only when absolutely necessary. If someone requests it, ask whether you can use a different form of identification. Don't write your Social Security number on checks or include it on any sort of application, unless required to do so and only when you trust the person and business requesting it.

- Shred or destroy any receipts, credit card receipts and statements, credit card applications, insurance forms, physician statements, and any other documents that contain your personal information before tossing them in the trash.

- Store personal records in a safe, secure location, especially if you frequently have guests or workers in your house or apartment.

- Pay attention to your billing cycles. If your bills don't arrive on time, contact the billing department and find out why.

(continued)

- Check your credit report regularly. You can obtain a free credit report online at *www.annualcreditreport.com* or by calling 877-322-8228. If any loans pop up on your credit report that you didn't apply for, report the incident to the credit reporting agency and to local law enforcement authorities.

- On the Internet, use a different user name and password for each site you choose to log on to. Change your password often.

- Every so often, head down to the county clerk's office or register of deeds, and check the deed on your home to make sure it's still in your name.

- Reduce the number of unsolicited telemarketing calls you receive by adding your name to the Do Not Call registry at *www.donotcall.gov*. If you do receive a telemarketing call after adding your name to the registry, you can be fairly certain that the person calling is not from a reputable company.

National Title, Inc., and Chicago Title Guarantee, Inc. TDF was supposedly set up to purchase the loans after Flagstar and IMPAC provided the initial funding; this made the loans a more attractive proposition for Flagstar and IMPAC. The two title companies were actually phony businesses simply set up to receive funds and lend an air of legitimacy to the operation.

When one of Flagstar's loan processors became suspicious, Flagstar began requiring copies of the loan applicants' driver's licenses. To get over this speed bump, Small began collecting copies of driver's licenses from employee files. When Small ran out of licenses to use, he directed one of his employees to place a false employment ad in the local newspaper claiming that Amerifunding was offering $100,000 per year for applicants with no prior experience. Each applicant, of course, had to submit a copy of his or her driver's license.

One of the job applicants learned that he had taken out a loan he didn't apply for when a loan processor at Flagstar called to tell him that she thought the loan was fraudulent. The applicant learned that a loan had been taken out in his name for $460,000!

How much Small and his associates profited from the fraudulent loans is debatable. According to the government's calculations, Small duped Flagstar and IMPAC out of more than $35,000,000. Small has claimed that the actual loss was a little over $2 million. Whomever you choose to believe, the fact is that Small and his cohorts stole a lot of money and ruined the credit histories of the many people whose identities they stole. Small is currently doing time in prison after pleading guilty to federal charges including bank fraud and wire fraud.

18

PREDATORY LENDING PRACTICES:

Bending and Breaking the Rules

L enders are more often the victims than the perpetrators of scams, and most lending institutions are fraud-free, but predatory lenders who are out to make a profit at the expense of less sophisticated, more desperate borrowers contribute their fair share to real estate fraud. They often soak unsophisticated borrowers with hidden fees and charges and saddle them with high-interest loans, making the money less affordable.

In this chapter, we describe the various methods that unsavory middlemen use to cheat borrowers, lenders, and the system. We provide case studies revealing predatory lending practices in action. We point out the warning signs you need to watch out for and explain the steps you need to take to avoid falling victim to predatory lending.

WHAT CONSTITUTES PREDATORY LENDING?

Predatory lenders often employ many of the same tactics used in the mortgage fraud schemes described elsewhere in this book. Loan officers, for example, may obtain inflated appraisals to get the borrower a higher loan or will falsify income information to qualify the borrower. Rather than doing this to help the borrower, predatory lenders are simply out for their own gain. Their actions rarely have any tangible benefits for the borrowers and often saddle the borrowers with loans they can't afford. Loan officers simply use the borrowers to engage in a type of fraud typically referred to as *fraud for commissions.*

Federal and state laws don't exactly identify "predatory lending" as a crime, but the practices are readily identifiable and include the following:

- Refinancing a mortgage repeatedly within a short period of time and charging higher than normal loan origination fees (including points) each time
- Selling a high-cost, high-interest loan to a borrower who would qualify for a lower-cost, lower-interest loan that the same lender offers
- Adding products or services to a loan without adequately informing the borrower about the need or cost of these products or services—such as credit life insurance
- Providing "products" that are nonexistent or offer no benefit
- Convincing loan applicants to borrow more than they can reasonably afford to pay back
- Pressuring loan applicants to accept high-risk loans such as balloon loans, interest-only mortgages, and loans with high prepayment penalties
- Selling high-interest loans to borrowers based on ethnicity or nationality rather than their credit history and financial situation

Hidden Loan Fees

One of the more subtle forms of predatory lending consists of charging higher than normal fees and including other products and services that are either nonexistent or simply offer no benefit to the borrower. These fees often include points, interest, and single premiums for credit life insurance. Although many of these same fees are included in any loan, predatory lenders may charge higher fees and include more "products" and "services" without properly informing the borrower in advance.

Approving Unqualified Applicants

Loan officers are often paid on commission. The more loans they sell, the more they make. In many cases, they can earn an even higher commission by selling high-cost loans and additional products and services. In other words, the motivation to make money sometimes eclipses a loan officer's responsibility to follow the rules.

The rules that loan officers are supposed to follow stipulate the parameters for approving and underwriting a loan. Although the stipulations may seem overly restrictive to some loan officers, the rules are in place for a reason—typically to make sure that the borrower can afford the monthly payments.

Lending guidelines and programs are designed to reduce the risk to both lenders and borrowers. The lender uses information on the loan application and gathers information from other sources to calculate the applicant's ability to make payments. The lender bases the approval on several factors, including the following:

- Household income
- Applicants' assets, including cash savings and real property
- Existing debt
- Applicants' credit history and FICO score (FICO is short for Fair Isaac Company, the creators of the index that many mortgage lenders use to determine a borrower's ability to repay a loan)

- Property's market value
- Whether the applicants will be living in the house they're buying (Borrowers are more likely to make payments on a house they're living in than on, for example, a summer cabin.)

The lender crunches the numbers, examines the facts, and determines the level of risk associated with the loan. If the risk is too high, the lender may simply reject the loan application. In situations with moderate risk, the lender may charge a higher interest rate to accommodate for the higher level of risk. In low-risk situations, the lender typically offers the borrower a lower interest rate. This protects the prospective borrowers from "getting in over their heads" and protects the lender's interests.

In many cases, a "helpful" loan officer will go out of her way to assist buyers in financing their dream homes, even though the buyers are unlikely to be able to afford the mortgage payments. If the loan officer is in a really helpful mood, she may actually change information on the loan documents or falsify documents to improve the borrowers' chances of qualifying for the loan. This "help," however, isn't very helpful. It raises the risk of the loan to the lender and places financial strain on the borrowers, often leading to foreclosure. The only party who's helped is the loan officer, who's helping herself to higher commissions.

Charging Undisclosed Origination Fees

Borrowers can usually find someone willing to loan them money, but they may have to pay a steep price for assistance in obtaining a loan. Some loan officers specialize in high-risk loans, and they make sure they get paid by charging extra up front—special fees for special services, typically about 1 to 5 percent of the total loan amount for the loan officer or broker to perform his magic. These are referred to as "advance fees," and in many instances the "loan officer" has no intention of obtaining a loan for the borrower and instead just takes off with the fee.

T*argeting* *and* S*teering*

Unethical loan officers often *target* borrowers based on race and nationality—people who may have trouble obtaining loan approval through traditional channels or may simply not be actively looking for loans.

In addition to targeting specific ethnic groups and nationalities, predatory lenders often target the following types of borrowers:

- Equity-rich, cash-poor homeowners
- Financially strapped homeowners who need money to pay their bills, cover medical expenses, get their cars repaired, or finance home improvements
- The elderly
- Low-wage earners

Suckering Borrowers with the Wrong Loan Products

Loan officers receive commissions based on not only loan balance but also the type of loan. Loans that carry higher interest rates result in higher commissions, giving loan officers the incentive to *steer* borrowers into the highest interest rate loan possible. Sometimes, borrowers who could otherwise qualify for "A" paper (lower interest) loans are placed in a costlier subprime loan simply because this will result in a higher commission for the loan officer.

Loan officers may also recommend an ARM (adjustable-rate mortgage) or an option ARM when the borrowers could qualify for a loan with better terms and a lower long-term interest rate. With an ARM, the interest rate may start low and then suddenly (or over some time) rise to a point at which the borrower can no longer afford the monthly payments. A loan officer may offer an ARM with a low "teaser" rate and then qualify the loan applicant based on the teaser rate rather than on the likely future payment amounts. When the interest rate jumps, the homeowner is either unable to make the

Spotting the Signs

Predatory lending is particularly sinister because professionals in a position of trust use that trust to con borrowers out of money. We encourage consumers to shop carefully for loans and remain aware of the following warning signs:

- The interest rate and terms on the loan documents at closing don't match what the loan officer presented when you applied for the loan.
- Your loan officer encourages you to fudge the facts on your loan application.
- Your loan officer instructs you to sign an application that contains blanks that he will later fill in or hurries you through the application process or closing, indicating that "you don't need to read everything."
- You feel pressured to apply for a loan for more money than you need.
- You're encouraged to take out a mortgage with higher monthly payments than you think you can reasonably afford.
- Someone tells you that you can't have copies of the documents you signed.
- You're told that you must purchase life insurance or disability insurance as a condition for the loan.

payments or must refinance the loan. This provides the loan officer with two opportunities to earn a commission—one off of the original loan and a second off of the refinance.

Bait and Switch

Mortgage brokers and loan officers may employ bait-and-switch techniques to fool borrowers or coerce them into taking out higher-cost loans. A broker or loan officer may present the borrower with a product, specifying the interest rate and monthly mortgage payment up front, and then change the terms just prior to closing. The borrowers show up at closing only to discover that the loan now has a higher interest rate, a prepayment penalty, or a balloon payment or has a negative amortization (meaning the principal of the loan will rise over the life of the loan).

Because borrowers are often up against tight deadlines or have structured their cash requirements around the presumption that the loan will close, the borrowers aren't always in a position to walk away from the closing table.

Loan Flipping and Churning

In chapter 7, we discuss illegal flipping—buying a house and then quickly reselling it for significantly more than its true market value. The terms *flipping* and *churning* mean something completely different when applied to loans. Flipping and churning consist of refinancing a loan over and over again to collect additional fees, including loan origination fees.

We've seen instances in which borrowers refinanced 10 to 20 times within a period of just a couple of years. Loan costs and commissions completely strip out all of the equity. Lenders don't benefit from this practice because they pay premiums to purchase the value of the interest stream and recoup those premiums only by receiving the payments of interest over the life of the loan. (Prepayment penalties are designed to insulate a lender from losses caused by early payoffs.) The loan officers and brokers who flip and churn are the only beneficiaries.

CASE STUDY

People who are determined to purchase a particular house often seek assistance from anyone who's willing to tell them what they want to hear and make it happen, even if "making it happen" is not in the buyers' best interest.

Recently, we learned of a case in which a real estate broker had advised a friend against purchasing a particular home. The broker examined his friend's finances and informed her that she couldn't possibly afford the house she wanted. The broker handed her a list of steps she could take to improve her financial situation so she could finance the purchase of a more affordable home in the future.

Six months later, the broker's friend told him that she had purchased a condo. She found a fabulous loan officer who worked with her to make her dream of homeownership come true. This "helpful" loan officer made the condo affordable through the following various creative financing maneuvers:

- Doctoring the loan application to make it appear as though she had a solid income
- Offering her an ARM with a low introductory interest rate
- Not setting up an escrow account to pay property taxes and insurance to keep the monthly payments low

Fourteen months later, her dream turned into a nightmare. The interest rate on the ARM jumped, and she was now paying $500 more per month than when she initially took out the loan. She couldn't afford to pay her property taxes and was facing foreclosure. She was unable to refinance because of her financial situation.

She returned to the helpful loan officer who told her he would figure out what to do. He was able to work out an 80/20 mortgage—two loans, one for 80 percent of the mortgage and another for 20 percent. To accomplish this, the loan officer had to artificially inflate the value of the property. The eager homeowner, however, remains financially strapped and has no equity in the property to protect her from any future financial setbacks.

Predatory lending has resulted in some well-publicized lawsuits and huge settlements. Following is a sample of cases that have made the headlines:

- In 2006, Ameriquest, the nation's largest subprime lender, agreed to pay $325 million to settle charges of predatory lending. Ameriquest was alleged to have pressured appraisers to inflate property values so borrowers could obtain higher-balance loans and to have imposed up-front fees without reducing interest rates as promised. Ameriquest employees allegedly told borrowers to ignore written information about interest rates, promising the company would give them lower rates later, but the company is alleged to have actually given them higher interest rates instead. Ameriquest was also accused of having assured some borrowers that their loans would have no prepayment penalties and then inserting penalties into the final loan documents; of having delayed the time period between the loan closing and the funding; and of misrepresenting fees and costs.

- In 2002, Household International agreed to change its practices and pay up to $484 million in consumer restitution for alleged predatory lending practices in the subprime market. Household was alleged to have overcharged borrowers fees and interest and misled borrowers about certain loan terms such as those concerning balloon notes and credit insurance.
- In 2002, Citigroup agreed to pay $240 million to resolve a Federal Trade Commission (FTC) lawsuit and class actions charging abusive-lending practices by The Associates, a subprime subsidiary it acquired in 2000. The FTC complaint alleged that The Associates engaged in deceptive practices designed to induce borrowers to unknowingly purchase optional credit insurance products—a practice known as "packing." The insurance products were intended to cover the borrowers' loan payments in various circumstances, such as death or illness, and the premiums were added to the principal amount of the loan. When consumers noticed that the credit insurance products were being added to the loan, Associates's employees used various tactics to discourage them from removing the insurance, the complaint alleged. The complaint also charged The Associates with additional deceptive practices and law violations.
- In 2002, First Alliance Mortgage agreed to a $60 million settlement with the FTC and with six states to resolve predatory lending complaints. The lawsuits alleged that First Alliance

Protect Yourself

Protecting yourself against predatory lending practices means that you need to become a savvy consumer. Take the following precautions whenever shopping or applying for a loan and when it's time to close on the loan:

- *Borrow from well-established lending institutions.* Don't trust companies who advertise with statements such as "No credit? No problem." Stick with traditional lenders.

- *Check references.* Before doing business with a mortgage broker or loan officer, make sure the person is a licensed broker or works for a licensed broker. Your state Banking Department should be able to provide this information. Also check with your local Better Business Bureau to make sure the person is in good standing.

- *Comparison shop.* Carefully check the interest rates and terms of at least three comparable loans from different lenders, and ask questions when you're unsure of what something means. Compare the annual percentage rates (APRs), fees, and points. Comparing loans often reveals red flags you may otherwise overlook.

- *Check for early payment penalties.* Early payment penalties can make it costly for you to refinance your loan if you find a more affordable loan later.

- *Read the paperwork.* Your lender should provide you with a Good Faith Estimate prior to your signing for the loan. Read it carefully and compare it against the loan documents (typically called the Settlement Statement or HUD-1) you receive at closing to make sure nothing has changed. Also, read the Truth in Lending statement carefully.

- *Prepare for closing.* Insist on receiving copies of the loan documents two to three days prior to closing so you can read them carefully before signing anything. If you have questions or concerns about any items on the closing documents, call the lender and have those issues resolved prior to closing.

- *Live within your means.* You know how much money you have, how much you earn, and how much you can afford to pay each month in loan payments. Don't let someone else convince you that you can afford a more expensive house or need to cash out the equity in your home to pay for a new car, a vacation, or other stuff you don't really need. Don't rely on representations that you will make more money next year or that the equity

(continued)

in your house will increase. These things don't necessarily happen, and if you take out a mortgage loan counting on a future event to occur, you could end up losing your home.

- *Take as much time as you need.* Don't let someone rush you through the signing of any legal documents. Take the time to read each document in its entirety—including the fine print. Obtaining the documents a few days prior to closing can provide you with the time you need without dragging out the closing.

- *Avoid suspicious lenders.* Lenders who show up at your door or contact you via phone or the Internet offering great deals on loans, same-day approval, or low interest rates if you "act now" are more suspicious than others. Don't sign anything or provide any sensitive personal information, such as your Social Security number.

- *Don't trust promises of future better terms or interest rates.* If someone tells you that you can't qualify for a more affordable loan now but that you can get a better loan later, after closing, don't believe it. The person is probably just setting you up to take out future loans to get another commission off of you later.

- *Consult trustworthy organizations.* If you believe that you're a victim of predatory lending or have additional questions about this subject, visit Freddie Mac's Don't Borrow Trouble website at *www.dontborrowtrouble.com*.

- *Don't sign loan documents that have blanks.* Write "NA" (not applicable) in any blank spaces so nobody can go back and fill in the missing information later.

marketed its loans through telemarketing and direct mail solicitations. Consumers who visited First Alliance's loan offices in response to the solicitation were subjected to a lengthy sales presentation known as the "Track." It was alleged that the solicitations and the "Track" presentation misled consumers about the existence and amount of loan origination fees or points and other fees, which typically amounted to 10 to 25 percent of the loan. Consumers also were allegedly misled about increases in the interest rate and the amount of monthly payments on ARM loans that the company offered.

19

LOAN SERVICING FRAUD— OR IS IT?

Once homeowners finance the purchase of a property, they enter into a 30-year relationship (or whatever term they agree to) with an entity known as a *loan servicer,* a middleman who processes the monthly mortgage payments and acts as the primary point of contact for the borrower. The loan servicer's job is to receive the monthly mortgage payments, manage any escrow account that has been set up to make property tax and homeowners' insurance payments, handle any necessary contact with the borrower, send the monthly mortgage payments to the lender, and keep records for the homeowners showing the annual payment amounts applied to principal and interest and paid out in taxes and insurance premiums. The loan servicer is also responsible for collecting late payments, managing delinquencies, and, if necessary, foreclosing on the collateral.

Loan servicers typically do a fairly good job of keeping the books on a home mortgage loan and making sure the lender, the property tax collector, and the homeowners' insurance company receive their payments. In some cases, however, certain loan administration policies have led to errors, such as failure to apply payments immediately after receipt, resulting in late payment penalties to borrowers. In a few extreme cases, irresponsible practices have even led borrowers into foreclosure.

This chapter provides a balanced view of the loan servicing industry, describing the relationship between the loan servicer, the borrower, and the lender. We describe certain questionable practices and the errors that may result in problems for the borrower and also provide a case study that reveals how some loan servicing practices can result in excess charges to borrowers. Throughout this chapter, you will learn the signs to watch out for and the preventive measures to implement to steer clear of trouble with loan servicers.

LOAN SERVICERS: GOOD AND BAD

Few lenders actually service their own mortgage loans. The lender owns the loan and the right to receive the payment stream but contracts with the loan servicer, giving the servicer the right and obligation to collect payments. Most homeowners think that they're sending their monthly mortgage payments to the bank from which they borrowed the money, when in fact they're paying the loan servicer, and the loan servicer is passing the payment along to the bank or other lending institution.

In the following sections, we describe the way that loan servicing is supposed to work and reveal some loan administration practices that can cause problems for homeowners.

The Role of the Loan Servicer

In addition to being responsible for properly processing your monthly mortgage payments, loan servicers are required by law to act in accordance with a consumer protection statute called Real Estate Settlement Procedures Act (RESPA). According to RESPA, which you can learn more about at *www.hud.gov,* loan servicers must abide by the following rules:

- *They must respond to questions and complaints within 60 days of receipt.* You must submit your request in writing separate from your payment.
- *They must notify you in writing at least 15 days before loan servicing is transferred to another company.* The notice must state the effective date of the transfer; include the name, address, and toll-free (or collect call) phone number of the new servicer; provide information on "whether you can continue any optional insurance, such as mortgage life or disability insurance, and what action, if any, you must take to maintain coverage"; and include a statement that the change of servicing does not affect the terms directly related to the servicing of your loan.
- *For a 60-day period beginning on the effective date of the transfer, the loan servicer must treat any late payments as on time if they're late because you sent them to the previous servicer.* In other words, you have about two months to get accustomed to sending payments to the new loan servicer.

Irresponsible Loan Servicing Practices

Various practices have resulted in successful lawsuits against loan servicing companies. The lawsuits generally fall into one of the following two categories:

1. *Violation of a statutory or other legal obligation that affects multiple borrowers.* These class action lawsuits filed against a lender on behalf of a large group of borrowers typically claim that payments were not being applied in a timely or correct manner—resulting in erroneous late payment charges or wrongful foreclosure.
2. *Specific misconduct by a loan servicer that affects a single borrower.* These individual lawsuits filed by a single borrower against

a loan servicer typically claim that the loan servicer failed to properly manage and record payments in a timely manner or failed to pay the lender or make required property tax payments and insurance premiums out of escrow.

But Is It Fraud?

Homeowners often confuse irresponsible practices and honest mistakes with fraud. If you search the Web for "loan servicing fraud," you're likely to find dozens of websites and blogs devoted to the topic. In most cases, the people complaining about loan servicing fraud are convinced that the big bad lenders are out to get them. They believe that the lenders manufacture loan defaults by intentionally mismanaging their accounts. In reality, we see very few cases in which a loan servicer intentionally mismanaged an account to force the borrower into paying penalties or to manufacture a foreclosure situation. Frankly, most "servicing fraud" is due to servicing errors or bad practices. This doesn't mean that the result for the borrower is any less severe. When loan servicing errors do occur, they can spiral very quickly from a $50 issue to foreclosure.

One argument we often hear is that lenders manufacture defaults when borrowers make partial payments. The borrower sends in a partial payment, and instead of immediately applying that partial payment, the loan servicer posts the payment to a suspense account and then continues to post later payments the same way even though the suspense account contains enough money to make a full payment. Servicers do this because if they were to accept the later payments, they would essentially be waiving their right to foreclose based upon the initial default. Servicers do not typically accept payment of part of what is owed on a loan unless the borrower has a forbearance agreement or other payment plan in place.

The servicer isn't processing payments in this way because they don't want the money or are simply being difficult. They do it because this is the only way they have to legally enforce their rights.

Spotting the **S**igns

Although we rarely observe situations in which loan servicers have crossed the line into committing bona fide fraud, as a homeowner, you should protect your rights by reading your mortgage statements and working with your loan servicer to correct any errors. Loan servicers are generally very large companies that handle tens of thousands of loan payments, and sometimes they make mistakes. Here are some of the warning signs that your mortgage payments are not being handled properly:

- Payments you made are not posted to your account.
- You have an escrow account from which property taxes and insurance premiums are to be paid, and these are not being paid or are being paid late.
- You're paying extra each month to pay down the principal on your mortgage, and the extra you're paying is not being applied to the principal.
- Your loan servicer charges you excessive late fees, home preservation or inspection fees, corporate advance fees, broker price opinion fees, or a forced placed insurance fee—such as homeowners' insurance purchased by the loan servicer—and there is no basis for these charges.

Otherwise a borrower could make partial payments every month (in violation of the loan agreement), and the lender could never foreclose. Borrowers who get behind on their payments in this way need to resolve the issue through the loss mitigation department of the loan servicer.

CASE STUDY

Issues with loan servicing continue to be addressed by the courts in case-by-case situations and through class actions filed by borrowers. Over the years, the obligations of loan servicers have been clarified,

High-Profile Loan Servicing Fraud

Unfair and deceptive loan servicing practices were discovered during the Federal Trade Commission's litigation against Capital City Mortgage Corporation (filed in U.S. District Court for the District of Columbia in January 1998). Capital City Mortgage originated and serviced subprime mortgage loans, and the FTC alleged that Capital City Mortgage Corporation included phony charges in monthly mortgage statements, added phony charges to loan balances, forced consumers to make monthly payments for the entire loan amount while withholding some loan proceeds, foreclosed on borrowers who were in compliance with the terms of their loans, and failed to release liens on borrowers' homes after the loans were paid off. A settlement, reached in February 2005, permanently enjoined the defendants from future deception, required them to pay consumer redress and other monetary relief, and required them to post a $350,000 performance bond to remain in the lending business.

(September 14, 2006, based on a letter from Donald S. Clark, Secretary, Federal Trade Commission, to Jennifer L. Johnson, Secretary, Board of Governors of the Federal Reserve System, re: Docket No. OP-1253)

and servicers have become more sensitive to abuses in the industry. Nevertheless, servicing problems still arise, such as the one described in this case study.

In 2002, a borrower reported that when her mortgage was transferred to a new loan servicing company, the new servicer requested proof of homeowners' insurance. She provided information over the phone, faxed her homeowners' insurance policy to the company, and even mailed in a copy of the policy. Over the course of six weeks, she had provided the requested information 11 times, and the loan servicer never responded.

On her next statement, she discovered a charge of $42 for "forced placed insurance." The loan servicer purchased homeowners' insurance for her and then billed her the premium. Eventually she was able to prove that she had insurance for the period covered by the forced placed insurance, and the charge was refunded.

Protect **Y**ourself

Even the most reliable loan servicers occasionally make mistakes, and there are certainly times when certain servicers have engaged in fraudulent or unethical practices. To protect yourself from being victimized by mistakes or irresponsible loan administration practices, implement the following preventive measures:

- Keep all records of your loan payments, including canceled checks, for the life of your loan. Payment histories are sometimes lost during a transfer to another servicing company, and you might be called on to prove that you made payments.

- Always review documents received from your mortgage servicer, particularly notices of when payments were posted and changes in escrow payment amounts and escrow balances.

- If your loan servicer provides online access to your account, sign up for it, and check your account every month to make sure your payments are being posted and that the right amounts are being applied to principal and interest and to your escrow account if you have one.

- If you believe you have been overbilled for escrow or other services by your servicer, it's a good idea to pay the fees, if you can afford them, even though you plan to dispute them. Mark the check "paid under protest," and then engage in a written dispute procedure with the servicer or file complaints with regulatory agencies. If you fail to make the payments, even though they are very small amounts, it can result in your entire mortgage loan being held delinquent and being placed into the foreclosure process, which can result in more and more fees. Although you may be right, it may take litigation to prove it, and losing your house in the process may not be worth it—even if you win a lawsuit against the servicer.

- If you talk on the phone with a representative of the loan servicing company, write down the name of the person and what she said, and follow up with a letter (and keep a copy of it) to confirm what you discussed. Written records are your best defense against poor memories.

Remember that information provided in this book or on any website or other publication does *not* take the place of legal advice. If you have fallen behind on your mortgage payments or have questions or concerns about your mortgage loan account, do not delay in seeking legal advice—the more delinquent your loan is when you seek assistance, the fewer options you may have. Filing a complaint against a loan servicer with the authorities or with a governmental agency is not a substitute for obtaining legal representation.

20

PROTECTING YOUR BUSINESS FROM FRAUD

People get flu shots to prevent the flu. They strap themselves into their cars with safety belts to avoid injury in the event of a car accident. They install antivirus software on their computers to block malicious software. Yet few businesses who have thousands or even millions of dollars to lose from real estate and mortgage fraud take the necessary precautions to properly educate their employees, clamp down on fraud, and punish the perpetrators.

Many real estate businesses, including mortgage brokers, title companies, lending institutions, appraisal companies, and real estate agencies, don't even give fraud a second thought—until it's too late. When the FBI comes knocking at your door, it's too late. When the grand jury subpoenas records and requests your employees to testify, it's too late. When state regulators seize your records and set up camp in your office to investigate fraudulent transactions, it's too late. When the name of your business is splashed across the front page of the local papers, your reputation is ruined, and nobody will do business with you, it's way too late.

As a business owner, you can act with all the goodwill and integrity in the world, but if you have one bad apple working for you or one employee who missed the fraud memo and training sessions, you're at risk, and you're not doing your best to protect the industry from which you and your employees earn a living.

This chapter shows how real estate business owners can become proactive to prevent real estate fraud before it happens. This chapter also shows how to clean house in the event that your business becomes involved in a fraudulent scheme, control the damage, and repair the valuable reputation of your business.

IMPLEMENTING POLICIES AND PROCEDURES TO PROTECT YOUR BUSINESS

Real estate and mortgage fraudsters have procedures in place to exploit vulnerabilities in the system. These vulnerabilities exist, at least in part, because real estate businesses fail to create and implement their own policies and procedures to foil the fraudsters.

Unfortunately, no single set of policies and procedures is sufficient for all businesses. In other words, we can't provide you with a step-by-step fraud prevention manual or a list of bullet points that can guarantee protection against fraud. However, we can provide you with the following guidelines and goals that should factor into the policies and procedures you develop:

- *Know why someone is likely to commit fraud.* Would an employee be likely to commit fraud for kickbacks, higher commissions, raises and promotions, or bonuses? Sometimes knowing the possible motivations can help you spot vulnerabilities, identify suspects, and remove some of the motivation. Commissioned employees are most likely to bend or break the rules for their largest sources of business—these are the highest source of risk for the business.

- *Minimize motivating factors.* You can minimize motivating factors in either of two ways: 1) remove the reward for committing fraud, or 2) increase the penalty for committing fraud.
- *Identify the opportunities for fraud in your system.* Where is fraud likely to occur in your business? Identify the gatekeepers who approve transactions. Identify the documents that may be more prone to forgeries and fabrications.
- *Build an atmosphere of integrity.* Businesses that bend the rules in their daily operations are more prone to becoming fraud centers. With no black-and-white ethical guidelines to follow, employees may see every issue as gray. They no longer have a line to cross because the line doesn't exist. Anything goes.
- *Implement a system of checks and balances.* The fewer people involved in a transaction, the more open it is to fraud. Transactions should be approved by one or more other individuals who've been sufficiently trained to spot and stop fraudulent transactions. The more eyes you have out looking for trouble, the more likely someone will spot it.
- *Check and cross-check identification.* Require that all employees who are responsible for receiving and processing signed documents carefully check the signer's identification. They should check the driver's license with a black light (to make sure it's not a cheap counterfeit) and cross-check the license against additional pieces of identification.
- *Take photos and thumbprints.* A digital camera behind the desk that films anyone who shows up to submit a document is an effective deterrent. Few criminals will perpetrate a crime when they know they're being filmed. Also consider having anyone involved in a transaction leave a thumbprint.
- *Audit files regularly.* A complete and detailed audit of all transactions that flow through your office is best. Spot-checking files is not quite as effective, but it's better than nothing. If you only spot check, audit a stratified random sample, ensure that random samples are attributable to different combinations of

Who's Responsible for Preventing Fraud in Your Business?

One of the tragically strange things about fraud prevention is that many businesses know about it but do absolutely nothing to practice it. Sheri Fitzpatrick, CEO, and Michael Blackburn, COO, of Perfect Home Living INC (*www.perfecthomeliving.com*) do an excellent job of relating just how prevalent this hands-off management policy really is when it comes to fraud:

"During a roundtable discussion we conducted with executive board members of a leading financial institution, we posed the question, 'Which position in your organization is your greatest liability?'

"The executives listed every imaginable job title as the weakest link. Not fully understanding the point of the exercise, board members quickly began blaming one another for everything from failed copiers to the poor performance of the mortgage division.

"Near the end of our session, we asked the members of the executive board to show, by raising a hand, who amongst them was involved in the daily matters of fraud prevention. Not one hand went up.

"Finally, we asked who in the room had recently spoken with or dealt directly with employees who were at the forefront of fraud prevention. Again, not one person in the room raised a hand.

"The point of the exercise was simply to show that none of the people running the company was actually involved in fraud prevention. They knew it was going on. They knew how much they were losing through fraudulent transactions, yet not one of them was actively involved in stopping it or even communicating with the people in-house who were in the best position to spot fraud. How could they possibly believe that the problem would go away?

"Employees form the frontline defense against real estate and mortgage fraud. They're the ones who have direct contact with the criminals and are often actively recruited to participate in fraud. Company executives and managers need to identify key personnel and properly educate and motivate them to expose any suspicious activity and criminal behavior.

"Many companies invest significant amounts of money on public relations campaigns to prove their value and integrity to consumers, but they often forget that one well-publicized incident of fraud can quickly destroy their public image. Don't let your company become a safe haven for real estate and mortgage fraud. Become proactive in preventing it from happening to your business."

employees, and include the files for your company's largest accounts or "best customers."

- *Perform background checks on prospective employees.* A background check can help you weed out the obvious (convicted) con artists, although it's certainly not 100 percent effective. Fraud often goes unreported because companies who report it are afraid that the criminal will file a lawsuit against them. The fraudster is free to move on to another company and continue perpetrating fraud, and they often do just that.

- *Educate employees.* No fraud prevention system can possibly be effective without trained personnel in place to implement it. Employees need to be able to spot the red flags of fraud and know exactly whom to contact to report suspicious activity without suffering any negative consequences. See "Educating Your Employees" and "Encouraging Whistle-Blowers" later in this chapter for details.

- *Designate two or more employees as fraud point persons.* Whenever an employee suspects fraud, the employee should be able to contact the point person who can then take the necessary action or contact a real estate and mortgage fraud consultant (kept on retainer) who can provide further guidance on how to proceed.

CASE STUDY

Nobody who runs a real estate business is immune to fraud. Even the most careful and vigilant employer may discover one of his employees participating in fraudulent transactions. A prominent real estate broker tells his story, changing the names to protect the identities of those involved:

"Martha joined our office after working at a title company. Martha was an underwriter so she reviewed documents prior to closing. She had an outgoing personality that made her a perfect candidate to work as a real estate agent. I knew she could be a top-selling agent so I asked her if she'd be interested in pursuing a career as a real estate agent. She accepted.

"Over the course of a couple years, Martha attended various real estate classes, received additional on-the-job training, and earned her license. She decided she wanted to specialize in working with investors, and she started selling foreclosures (HUD, VA, and real estate owned [REO] properties) and distressed homes. Eventually, she hooked up with a guy named Mike, who was offering real estate investment seminars and selling his programs online.

"What Mike would do is make an offer on a house to buy it from an REO broker, which is a broker who sells houses for lenders who foreclose on homes and ultimately take possession of them. Mike would claim to be offering cash for the houses, but he was actually only tying them up (without cash) and then selling them.

"With only about one year of experience, Martha was able to sell 17 houses in a single month—that's an impressive number of houses for even a seasoned pro, and it looked as though she was going to be selling even more houses the following month.

"In Martha's enthusiasm, she shared information with another agent, Phil, who headed our foreclosure acquisition department, and tried to convince him to do a transaction. Phil gathered all the information and reported it to management. At the same time, another participant tried to convince me that 'everyone was doing it.' One of my listing managers and another agent were working on a transaction with Martha and a seasoned client. I told them not to proceed because what they were planning was not legal.

"I became distracted during my father's illness and ultimate death. During that time, these three met with a mortgage broker who convinced them that the deal was on the up-and-up, and before I knew it, they closed on the deal. I retained our private investigator, a former police commissioner, to review our findings and turn the matter over to the authorities.

"I gathered the files on the houses that Martha had sold and quickly saw that all of the transactions used a straw buyer—or a straw LLC (limited liability corporation). The organizers of the scam were tying up the properties being sold by the REO brokers through the LLC and then selling those houses at inflated prices—illegally flipping the houses. They were using Martha so they would have our company's name on the transactions to make them appear legitimate.

"I don't know if Martha was questioning the transactions, but the organizers of the scam decided that they needed to offer Martha an additional perk for her continued cooperation. They found out that Martha was getting married and offered to help her and her new husband by selling them one of the houses and providing $40,000 cash back at closing. Often, the fraud organizers find a cooperative insider and then suck them in by providing some tempting form of compensation. They try to get as many professionals actively involved in the illegal activity so they can surround themselves with people who can make the scheme appear legitimate and won't turn them in. Another person they recruited was an appraiser who agreed to inflate multiple appraisals in exchange for some cash back at closing.

"By the time I found out about it, Martha and her new husband had closed on five transactions and received more than $100,000 in cash back proceeds. One of the funny aspects of this case is that Martha's husband was a local law enforcement officer. He personally attended only one of the closings. He signed a power of attorney over to Martha so she could sign for him at the other closings.

"When we confronted Martha and explained that these deals were fraudulent, she wouldn't believe me, my assistant, or our managers. I invited the IRS, FBI, and one of the local sheriffs to my office to discuss real estate fraud. During the meeting, I brought up the situation concerning Martha. Together, we marched down to Martha's office to explain to her she was involved with fraud. That's when she began to realize that what I had been telling her all along was true. She was in deep trouble and was now very concerned for her husband (who knew nothing about it) and the future of his career."

EDUCATING YOUR EMPLOYEES

As a real estate professional, you and anyone working for you is a guardian of the American dream of homeownership. Your responsibility is to protect the homeowner and the industry from the opportunistic parasites who feed off that dream and suck money from the system. Make sure your employees understand that ignorance of the law is no excuse, and then provide them with the training required to spot shady deals and sound the alarm. Training should highlight the following key points:

- Looking the other way or choosing not to get involved is not an option. It simply makes you a silent partner.
- Define fraud and provide detailed descriptions of the types of fraud that your employees are likely to witness. The descriptions presented in this book provide an excellent start. As new schemes and scams surface, we will continue to post them on *FlippingFrenzy.com* and *MortgageFraudBlog.com*.
- Highlight the red flags that often accompany a fraudulent transaction so your employees know what to look for.
- Distribute fraud alerts so employees are aware of the latest schemes they may encounter.
- Provide all employees, from entry level to CEOs, with fraud training from an expert in real estate and mortgage fraud who has insider experience in all areas. Make this training a requirement in your office, company, region, division, and so on.

Ending the Conspiracy of Silence

Real estate and mortgage fraud has been a raging epidemic for several years, but the real estate industry has chosen to try to sweep it under the rug in the hopes that it will magically disappear.

Real estate professionals are often reluctant to publicize abuses of the system for various reasons, including the following:

- Lenders are hesitant to report it because they don't want stockholders to lose trust. Any hesitancy that might exist in federally regulated financial institutions is counter-balanced by the reporting requirements because failure to file required Suspicious Activity Reports can result in significant fines.

- Many real estate professionals avoid reporting fraud because they're afraid that legislators will pass a host of new regulations that will complicate their lives and start examining their dirty laundry. This fear factor needs to be eliminated. Just saying "no" is not enough—professionals have to spot it, stop it, and post it!

- As property values soar due to inflated appraisals, everyone in the industry is making more money, especially the agents who receive higher sales commissions.

- As property values decline due to the economy, real estate professionals and home-sellers feel increased pressure to employ creative sales strategies, such as cash back at closing.

- Homeowners who receive cash back at closing are raking in the dough and sleeping well at night thinking that it's perfectly okay.

People are reluctant to accuse anyone of committing a crime because, in our society, the perpetrator is liable to turn around and file a lawsuit against the accuser for libel.

Lenders are very much aware of the problem and are often the biggest losers so they tend to be more proactive in the mortgage fraud arena. In 2006, the MBA (Mortgage Bankers Association) held a conference in Chicago dedicated to mortgage fraud. They made arrangements to accept 200 attendees, and it sold out immediately! In contrast, in 2005, the NAR (National Association of REALTORS®) reserved a room for 2,000 people and brought in a fraud expert from the FBI. Eighteen hundred seats were left empty. Real estate and mortgage fraud

(continued)

classes don't teach real estate agents how to make loads of money so nobody wants to attend voluntarily. The only ones attending are those who don't really need to be there—the people who already understand what's going on and want to rid the industry of fraud.

To succeed at curbing the rash of real estate and mortgage fraud, the entire industry needs to break the conspiracy of silence, and all professionals in the industry need to receive fraud training from real estate and mortgage fraud experts with professional insider experience.

- Encourage all employees, salespeople, and managers to sound the alarm if their instinct tells them that something isn't right. Many times, employees don't trust their own instinct and are reluctant to say anything. Foster an environment in which employees are not worried about sounding false alarms.
- Clearly present the rules that employees need to follow and the consequences that will occur if the employee doesn't follow those rules. Strictly and consistently enforce the rules so all employees know you're serious.

BECOMING A PERCEPTIVE OBSERVER

Businesses should be able to trust their employees, but blind trust is not the most prudent approach. Stay connected with your employees and be observant. If you have an employee who's earning $75,000 a year and supporting a family of four and she drives up in a fancy new BMW one day, don't simply shrug it off as your employee's good fortune. Look into anything that seems out of the ordinary. Even the most trustworthy employees sometime succumb to the temptations of quick-cash opportunities.

You don't have to confront a suspected employee immediately, but you should remain observant and investigate any suspicions to ensure that your employee is not engaged in some fraudulent activity and using your business to do it. Don't fall asleep at the wheel.

ENCOURAGING WHISTLE-BLOWERS

Real estate and mortgage fraud are often silent crimes, but they're not victimless crimes. Your employees need to be made aware of the fact that these crimes harm real people and make housing less affordable for everyone. Often, businesses unknowingly, and sometimes knowingly, reward their employees for looking the other way and punish them for pointing out suspicious activities. A mortgage broker, for example, often bases bonuses and commissions on the volume of loans a particular loan officer brings in. Motivated by higher commissions, the loan officer is more susceptible to making bad decisions and even becoming a willing participant in fraud. Bonuses and commissions should be based on the success of their portfolio (the good loans they bring in), not on how many loans they sell.

Carefully review the system of rewards you use to motivate your employees and make sure you offer rewards for vigilance and whistle-blowing as well as for the volume of business your employees bring in. Also, make it easier for employees to point out suspicious activity. Let them know that their suspicions will be gratefully received and that they will be rewarded for their vigilance and for taking action. Don't put up with fraud harassment—don't allow other employees to harass the person who reported the incident. Setting up a tip line, email account, or other way for employees to anonymously report suspicious activity is also helpful. Employees usually know or suspect when fraud is occurring but have no way to inform management without alienating friends and coworkers.

PUNISHING THE PERPETRATORS

Unfortunately, real estate and mortgage fraud have become so rampant that the government has been forced to limit the amount of time and resources they can invest in investigating and prosecuting these cases. The con artists are able to perpetrate more fraud than law enforcement can keep up with.

To be effective, the system of punishment must become more of a grassroots effort. As a business owner, executive, or manager, you must enforce the rules by taking proper action, such as the following:

- Report incidents of fraud to your local law enforcement agencies and the FBI.
- Fire employees who participate in fraudulent activities.
- Report guilty employees to your state or federal governing (licensing) agency.
- Consult your attorney to find out if you can legally contact someone who hires an employee you fired for committing fraud. If you can legally inform the employer of the person's past conduct, do it.
- Consult your attorney about bringing a civil lawsuit against an employee who committed fraud. In addition to helping you collect some form of recovery, a lawsuit creates a public record that you may be able to share with the employee's future prospective employers and that you can point to if you and your company are accused of being involved in the fraud.

RECOVERING FROM AN UNFORTUNATE INCIDENT

Fraud happens even in businesses that are careful to avoid it. If you're lucky enough to discover fraud before the local or national news media gets hold of the story, you can often work with law enforcement to turn in the guilty parties and mitigate losses before the reputation of your business takes a hit. If the story does break, then take decisive action and lots of it. Of course, consult with your attorney about the situation first and only consider the following suggestions upon the advice and consent of your attorney:

- Fire the perpetrator as publicly as possible. Don't be the fall guy or gal for someone else's crime.

- Consult your real estate and mortgage fraud expert—someone you could retain to provide guidance and advice. Work with your consultant—if this is happening in your office, it's probably happening elsewhere. Get the word out there.
- Don't hide your head in the sand. If one of your employees committed fraud, consider admitting it.
- Don't try to cover it up. Get all the facts out in the open. The more you try to cover it up, the more determined the reporters will be to get the story out there.
- Hire a publicist to repair the damage to your business's reputation.
- Make sure the community is aware of all the facts. People often base their harshest judgments on sketchy details. The facts may help them change their perception of you and your business.

A fraud resource professional will soon become as essential as an attorney, human resource person, or bookkeeper. In most cases, this won't be your corporate attorney. When you think about how much you stand to lose from fraud or by having a fraudster working inside your company and ruining its reputation, you will soon learn that the expense is well worth it.

Chapter

21

FIXING THE SYSTEM

Con artists will always find ways to exploit vulnerabilities in the system, but the system can fight back. This chapter reveals how everyone involved in real estate—from buyers and sellers to real estate professionals to law enforcement officers and regulators all the way up to government officials—can work together to close the loopholes and make the system less vulnerable to fraud. By being honest and vigilant and by advocating for positive change at all levels, we can crowd out the con artists, making it nearly impossible for them to operate.

FIGHTING BACK WITH EDUCATION

The most effective defense against fraudsters and con artists is education. By arming everyone who has a stake in the real estate and mortgage industries and in preserving the American dream of homeownership with the knowledge and skills they need to spot and stop fraudulent real estate transactions, we can begin to take back that American dream from the forces who are actively working to destroy it.

The con artists and their coconspirators are well schooled. They're fully aware of how the system works and how to exploit the vulnerabilities in the system. They're often very highly skilled with computers and the Internet and have all the tools required to counterfeit documents, steal identities, and fudge credit histories. And they're usually well connected to professional insiders who can lend credibility to the fictions they create to milk the system.

To fight back against these well-schooled, well-connected, and technically savvy fraudsters, we need to become equally well schooled and well connected and learn to use the tools of technology to carefully scrutinize documents, ask the right questions, and shut down shady deals before they happen.

Educating Consumers

Whether they're sellers or buyers, consumers are the "eyes on the ground." To protect their interests and become effective whistle-blowers, consumers need to know both the methods used to perpetrate fraud and the laws that govern real estate transactions. Essentially, consumers need to take personal responsibility for their own finances and for the role they play at the closing table. Failure to do so leaves consumers wide open to the risk of becoming victims or accomplices.

If you're a consumer, make a commitment to play an active role in every real estate transaction in which you're involved. Brush up on these essential words of advice:

- The lender must be provided with full disclosure of all financial details related to the transaction. If any information on the loan documents (including the loan application and HUD-1 Settlement Statement) is false or misleading to the lender from whom the money is being borrowed, the transaction is fraudulent. Don't listen to anyone who tries to tell you otherwise.

- Sometimes the lies are hard to spot, such as with cash back at closing schemes in which the purchase price is increased to cover concessions or kickbacks.
- Ask yourself this question: "If the buyer wasn't getting a loan, would there be any reason to structure the sale this way or raise the sales price?" If the answer is no, chances are good that you're dealing with a situation involving mortgage fraud.

Retraining Real Estate Professionals

Real estate professionals are highly motivated to commit fraud. Take a moment to consider all the motivation built into the system:

- An increased number of real estate transactions, including fraudulent transactions, generates more business for everyone.
- Illegal kickbacks deliver instant cash.
- Refusing to participate in fraudulent schemes often results in a loss of business.
- Clients, both buyers and sellers, pressure professionals to participate in fraudulent transactions or at least "look the other way." Professionals often break the law for their best clients. But when asked theoretically which of their clients they would be willing to go to jail for, we've never had a real estate professional come up with a single name!
- Everybody's doing it. Well, not everyone, but enough people are profiting from fraud to make it a highly attractive proposition.

Money attracts thieves. The real estate industry has plenty of money to go around, and real estate professionals are the first in line to receive their cut. When the market is hot, they devise tricks to increase their sales volumes and their profits, and when the market slows, they employ other tricks to generate sales and commissions.

Most real estate professionals know better. They know that lying on a loan application is wrong. They know that asking an appraiser to artificially inflate an appraisal is wrong. They even know that looking the other way is wrong. Their parents and teachers drilled the lessons of morality and ethics into them when they were young. What has happened, however, is that the culture of the industry and many of their mentors inside the industry have managed to train the ethics right out of them.

Real estate professionals learn from other real estate professionals, and right now, they're learning everything wrong. They're learning that fraud is just part of the business. Questionable and criminal practices, such as creating phony gift letters and using straw borrowers, are incorporated into everyday real estate transactions to the point at which illegal activities become the norm rather than the exception, and anyone who doesn't join the party is looked down upon as a sucker or a snob.

Real estate professionals need to be retrained legally, morally, and ethically, and with all the motivation to commit fraud working against us, we have only a couple of options to provide this training to those who need it most. To affect change, it is important to do the following:

- *Strictly discipline the real estate professionals who participate in fraudulent transactions.* We need to send a message to the industry that "everybody does it" is not a valid legal defense. Jail time, loss of license, and loss of proceeds from fraudulent deals will send the message loud and clear.
- *Make fraud training mandatory rather than voluntary.* The only people attending fraud training seminars are lenders (who have the most to lose) and real estate professionals who are already concerned and well aware of the problem—not the professionals who are perpetrating fraud.
- *Create an army of defenders of the American dream of homeownership.* The more people we can train to spot, stop, and post incidents of fraudulent real estate transactions, the greater deterrent we have against those who attempt to commit fraud and the greater motivation we create for those professionals to seek fraud training voluntarily.

Educating Law Enforcement

Most law enforcement officers are experienced and skilled in dealing with high-profile crimes including violent crime, theft, and vandalism. They're much less skilled in dealing with white-collar crimes, including identity theft and real estate and mortgage fraud. If a bank robber holds up a bank and scrams with $50,000, several squad cars show up almost immediately. Reporters rush to the crime scene. Details about the suspect are immediately distributed to all law enforcement agencies and broadcast on the local and sometimes national news. But when someone steals $50,000 at the closing table, you don't hear a peep.

Part of the problem is that white-collar crime has somewhat of a low profile. Crimes occur primarily on paper and online, cash is exchanged via wire transfers, and many of the witnesses are actively involved or have little motivation to report the crimes. Complicated schemes that unfold over the course of several days or even weeks and involve large quantities of complex legal documents are difficult to investigate. Often, law enforcement agents have little knowledge of the role each person plays in a transaction, who is responsible for receiving and reviewing each document, and what sort of checks and balances are in place. Without a firm understanding of these issues, investigating and prosecuting a real estate fraud can seem daunting.

To effectively investigate and prosecute these crimes, law enforcement agencies need to work directly with experienced real estate and legal professionals who have a detailed knowledge of real estate transactions and how the fraudsters operate. We work with law enforcement officers across the country, explaining the transactions and helping them to direct their investigations so as not to waste time and resources. Law enforcement agencies are beginning to take these crimes seriously and officers are gaining both experience and insight, but many agencies have not received funding for the training and resources they need.

PASSING AND ENFORCING LAWS

When you look at the rampant fraud in the real estate industry, the natural inclination is to ask, "Well, why doesn't somebody pass a law?" That's the inclination of most lawmakers, too. The fact is we already have laws that, if they were consistently enforced and well publicized, could put a huge dent in the incidence of real estate and mortgage fraud. For example, it's illegal to lie on a 1003 Uniform Residential Loan Application, which borrowers must fill out to apply for a loan, but that doesn't stop applicants from lying. In fact, many loan officers encourage applicants to lie on the form, or the loan officer simply fills in the blanks with false information after the applicant signs the form.

It's also a violation of appraisal standards for an appraiser to target her appraisal to the desired value of a property. An appraiser hired to perform an appraisal for loan purposes (particularly for a federally secured loan) can't simply tell a client, "If the appraisal is too low, just give me a call, and I'll rework the numbers." However, we've recently witnessed appraisers who were openly advertising this practice to generate more business.

The first step in using the law to crack down on real estate and mortgage fraud is to start enforcing the laws that are already on the books.

State Laws

Until 2005, there was no state or federal crime called "mortgage fraud." Cases of mortgage fraud were generally prosecuted by states under various different fraud, forgery, and theft statutes. That all changed when Georgia passed the first mortgage fraud statute on May 5, 2005. Known as the Georgia Residential Mortgage Fraud Act, this statute criminalizes any misrepresentation made to a lender for the purpose of obtaining credit in connection with residential real estate. The first arrests under the act happened quickly, and other states soon proposed similar legislation. At the time of this writing, at least eight other states have similar legislation pending: Arizona, Colorado, Illinois, Michigan, Mississippi, New Jersey, Texas, and Utah.

Other forms of real estate fraud primarily targeting consumers, including foreclosure rescue schemes, are typically prosecuted by state attorneys general or local law enforcement (county district attorneys). Some of these practices are not strictly illegal and are handled by the attorneys general on a civil level—for instance, by lawsuits for injunctions based upon unfair business practices. In most states, we need stronger consumer protection laws for homeowners in foreclosure, but we also need to protect the homeowners' rights to dispose of their property and pursue other options to retain the equity in their homes. In other words, we don't want laws that are too restrictive.

Some well-meaning legislatures have passed laws prohibiting the sale of property while the borrowers are in foreclosure unless a certain amount of value is returned to the owners. While these laws would seem to protect the consumer, they can actually be very damaging because homeowners may be unable to sell their property for enough to obtain the return that the statutes require. While it may seem like a good idea to make sure the homeowners aren't taken advantage of, for homeowners facing foreclosure, some money is often better than none. Selling the home at less than market value can help them avoid a serious blemish on their credit history. As with all areas, the competing and often conflicting needs of the various parties involved must be balanced to achieve workable solutions.

Lawmakers need to stop trying to merely plug the holes in the dam that's ready to break. They should consult the industry they are trying to govern so that the consumers' and homeowners' best interests are protected without placing additional constraints on already distressed homeowners.

Federal Laws

Several federal statutes already address the criminal aspects of mortgage fraud, and federal prosecutors have sufficient tools to adequately prosecute these crimes. The Uniform Residential Loan Application, for example, contains a statement that lying on the application is a federal crime and refers to the relevant federal statute:

> "I/We fully understand that it is a federal crime punishable by fine or imprisonment, or both, to knowingly make any false statements concerning any of the above facts as applicable under the provisions of Title 18, United States Code, Section 1001, et seq."

In addition, the activities engaged in during a fraudulent transaction are often separately indictable under the federal wire fraud, mail fraud, bank fraud, and money laundering statutes.

In 2006, Senators Barack Obama (D-Ill) and Dick Durban (D-Ill) introduced the "Stopping Transactions which Operate to Promote Fraud, Risk, and Underdevelopment Act" or the "STOP FRAUD Act" (S.2280), calling for a sweeping set of federal reforms to combat mortgage fraud, ratchet up enforcement, and create a national database of brokers who have been disciplined. The bill was never passed, which is not entirely a bad thing. The bill was aimed at fraud perpetrated by real estate professionals and did not address all aspects of real estate and mortgage fraud. Besides that, we already have plenty of antifraud laws that are not being enforced. The bill certainly received a lot of media attention, but failed to address significant issues. We expect to see more government discussion of the problem in future elections because efforts to protect the American dream of homeownership are beginning to increase.

Enforcing Current Laws

Increased legislation and regulation are certainly helpful, but without additional funding to provide regulators and law enforcement agencies with the training and resources required to enforce the ever-growing law books, we will find ourselves fighting a losing battle. Given the resources and permission to bring the perpetrators to justice, law enforcement agencies and professional organizations will be able to do their jobs more effectively. We recommend the following steps:

- With the proper training and resources, law enforcement will be better equipped to investigate fraud allegations and more effectively prosecute the fraudsters.
- Real estate and mortgage fraud experts in each county could be organized into task forces to work with the sheriffs' deputies and assist local law enforcement agencies.
- Professional organizations can discipline members who choose to participate in fraud by revoking licenses and certificates and working with law enforcement to charge and prosecute those members.
- Cross-agency enforcement may also be useful in cases in which real estate professionals try to induce their colleagues to engage in unethical or illegal practices. Of course, the person who actually commits the crime needs to be disciplined, but mortgage brokers, loan officers, and real estate agents who, for example, pressure an appraiser to inflate an appraisal should also be held accountable for their actions. Appraisal regulators don't have authority over these individuals because these individuals don't have appraisal licenses. Likewise, mortgage regulators don't address the conduct because there are no express prohibitions against third parties pressuring appraisers. Cross-agency enforcement may be able to address these enforcement limitations.

Real estate professionals need to see their peers being raided, indicted, prosecuted, and convicted for these offenses. Consumers who participate in fraudulent transactions should also be brought to justice. And the media ought to do more to publicize the problem and report on convictions to create a meaningful deterrent to committing such crimes.

Making the **P**unishment **F**it the **C**rime

Not all fraudsters are hardened criminals intentionally committing crimes. Sure, we see plenty of those, but many who commit real estate or mortgage fraud are average citizens who are lulled into thinking that what they're doing is not wrong, convinced that they will never be prosecuted, and duped into thinking that lenders don't really care if they bend the rules. The crooks who intentionally commit crime for profit need to be dealt with harshly so that they don't see real estate fraud as a low-risk, high-reward activity.

Judicial sentencing discretion is necessary, however, so that those who engage in less egregious conduct can be dealt with fairly. Making them pay back their ill-gotten gains would certainly be a start. Bringing these folks up on fraud charges in a courtroom would also serve as a wake-up call and a powerful deterrent.

CLEANING UP THE REAL ESTATE INDUSTRY FROM THE INSIDE OUT

Tragically, the people who make their living off of real estate and can do the most to stop fraud seem to be the least willing to stop it. We need to realize that the health of our businesses depends on the health of the industry. If we allow the fraudsters to bleed billions of dollars from the industry, the day will soon come when the entire housing market will collapse and all of us will be forced into making a career change.

In the following sections, we recommend some reforms that may be able to help curb fraud and restore the health of the real estate industry. As insiders, our preference should be to clean up our industry ourselves before the government cleans it up and burdens us with excess regulations. By making a few adjustments in the way you do business, you can do your part to clean up the real estate industry from the inside out.

MLS (Multiple Listing Service)

The MLS is a great tool for marketing and selling houses, but it's also a tool that con artists fully exploit. We have multiple MLSs that don't share data. This is a problem because when a real estate agent, on behalf of a seller, first lists a property for sale, they usually set an asking price in line with market values. When the listing attracts little buyer interest, the natural inclination is to reduce the asking price. However, when con artists see that the house isn't selling, they may decide that a better option is to *raise* the asking price and offer the buyer cash back at closing or some other valuable kickback for agreeing to purchase the overpriced property. If the seller's agent were to change the asking price on the same MLS from say $1.1 million to $3.3 million, the listing would obviously generate some suspicion. So the seller's agent simply lists the new price on a different MLS. In this case, the con artist walks away with his cut of the $2 million profit, free and clear. (The practice of raising listing prices in the MLS has been relied on by authorities as evidence in recent indictments of real estate agents in cash back at closing schemes!)

A national MLS may seem extreme, but if such a system were in place, significantly raising the asking price for a property would certainly draw suspicion and cause the fraudster to think twice about trying it. At the very least, MLSs should find a way to work together and share data to place an obstacle in the way of the fraudsters.

Buyers and Sellers

Buyers and sellers often fail to understand the closing documents they're signing. And who can blame them? The paperwork is often overly complicated and packed with language that requires an attorney to decipher. Proposed laws and regulations often call for adding even more complexities. Perhaps the following suggestions for simplifying and standardizing the forms would be more effective:

- Reduce and simplify the documentation to present borrowers with the important elements of the transaction in a way that's easy for them to understand.
- Standardize Good Faith Estimates so borrowers can more easily compare the overall costs of different loans.
- Require that any additional legislation regarding consumer protection take into account existing legislation and work toward streamlining the process rather than simply adding another disclosure to the stack that is already too voluminous to read and too complicated to understand.
- Highlight the fine print on the Uniform Residential Loan Application so borrowers are aware that lying on the application is a criminal offense.
- Provide the seller and the buyer a mandatory statement at closing informing them of the illegality of practices such as silent seconds and cash back at closing schemes.

Real Estate Agents

Real estate agents are required to take fair-housing training to ensure that they and their clients don't exclude buyers based on race, sex, religion, or other differences, but they are not yet required to take classes on real estate and mortgage fraud. To curb agent involvement in real estate and mortgage fraud, we suggest the following:

- Require real estate and mortgage fraud training for all real estate business owners, agents, managers, regional directors, independents, and franchises large and small. All licensing training and continuing education should include information on fraud.
- Require fraud certification. An agent can already obtain Graduate, Realtors Institute (GRI) certification. We propose a new certification of Graduate, Fraud Institute (GFI) so consumers and industry professionals can distinguish agents who are properly trained in real estate and mortgage fraud.

- Require that any proposed legislation that addresses pressuring appraisers to inflate appraisals also encompasses pressure exerted by real estate agents.
- Encourage industry publications, including REALTOR® *Magazine* (one of the largest industry publications), to regularly publish articles and information related to real estate and mortgage fraud.
- Fine real estate brokers when any of their agents is found guilty of participating in fraudulent transactions. A minimum fine of the amount the agent "earned" in commissions would encourage brokers to police their own agents.
- Require peer reviews so agents could assist in policing one another.
- Require that all documents from start to finish be scanned electronically and forwarded to each professional, including the lender, involved in the transaction to ensure that everyone has seen and reviewed the documents prior to closing. This can virtually eliminate the chance that extra addendums will be added after the documents are submitted to the lender.

Appraisers

As discussed in chapter 4, inflated appraisals play a major role in various scams. Requiring fraud certification and higher bonds would resolve much of the problem, but a national appraisal database along with some additional checks and balances could encourage less biased appraisals. Some suggestions include:

- Automate the system to highlight appraisals on houses that have transferred ownership three or more times in a span of three years and have increased in value beyond a certain reasonable percentage.
- Automate the system to send a confirmation to the appraiser who supposedly performed the appraisal, just in case someone is filing appraisals using a stolen identity.

- Automate the system to raise a red flag when more than one appraisal has been ordered in a short period of time.
- Send the appraisal history to the client, so the client is immediately aware of any sudden, extreme increases in appraised value.
- Require peer reviews of appraisers' work. This is standard practice with certified public accountants.
- Warn lenders not to forgo appraisal reviews by allowing drive-by appraisals or BPOs (broker price opinions).
- Encourage all national appraisal publications to carry a monthly fraud column both in print and online.
- Require that lenders verify appraisal details directly with the appraiser or obtain a duplicate copy of the appraisal directly from the appraiser when using an appraisal obtained through a third-party originator. If the third-party originator objects, the lender should not rely on the appraisal.
- Disallow loan originator involvement in the ordering of appraisals.

Notaries

Forged and counterfeit documents commonly play a role in real estate and mortgage fraud, and notaries form the front line of defense in these areas. Given the right to notarize documents is a privilege that's not to be taken lightly. To make notarization of documents less susceptible to abuse, we recommend the following:

- Requirements for becoming a notary should be much stricter. In some areas, becoming a notary is easier than getting a cash advance at an ATM.
- Notaries should have an electronic system that captures the signer's information (thumbprint and driver's license) and verifies the information.
- Notaries should be required to pass a fraud-certification test.

- A notary's thumbprint should be included on the notarized document or within the seal. (Notaries often claim that they are the victims of identity theft. Requiring a thumbprint would help prevent that from occurring.)
- Notaries should receive newsletters in print or electronically keeping them informed of their responsibilities and any new fraud schemes that may exploit the powers of a notary.
- Notaries should be legally prohibited from notarizing real estate or loan documents for family members.
- Notaries should be legally prohibited from notarizing documents in transactions in which they have a direct or indirect beneficial interest. (Most states prohibit notaries from notarizing documents in transactions in which the notary has a direct interest but provide no wording dealing with indirect interests.)
- An additional witness should be required to verify the identity and signatures of those signing the documents and then sign as a witness.
- Notaries should be required to obtain the thumbprint of the signatory in all transactions involving real property. (This requirement has currently been adopted only in California.)
- Notaries should be provided with the legal discretion to refuse to notarize a document if the notary believes that the signer is under duress or the victim of fraud.
- All states should mandate that notarial logs be maintained.

Many states already have rules and regulations that govern notaries, but often these rules are minimum standards and there are additional steps that notaries can and should take to protect themselves and the public. Under no condition should a notary be allowed to notarize a document that contains blank spaces to be filled in later.

Lenders

When you consider that the lender is often the only party at the closing table who doesn't have representation, it's no surprise that lenders are often the victims of mortgage fraud. When approving a loan, all they have to go on is a stack of paperwork with signatures. They're not privy to all the deals the other parties are making on the side.

Con artists often take a shotgun approach to fraudulent loans. They buy or steal a property and then submit several loan applications to obtain multiple loans on the same property. One way to put an end to this practice and less brazen attempts at mortgage fraud is for the lenders to set up a national database in which all loan applications are recorded. The database could be automated to sound the alarm when any of the following suspicious activities occur:

- Multiple loan applications are submitted using the same property as collateral.
- The appraised value of a property as stated on a loan application rises by a certain unreasonable percentage in a short period of time.
- A borrower seeks loans for multiple properties closing in a short period of time.
- The loan application fails to disclose other owned properties or applications in process.
- Loan applications submitted to different lenders within a prescribed period contain materially different information concerning the borrower.

Of course, any such database would need to address legal issues, including privacy.

Loan Officers

Well-qualified loan officers who balance the interests of both of their clients—lenders and borrowers—are certainly the norm rather than the exception, but far too many loan officers are more motivated by sales and commissions than they are by ethics. Unethical loan officers often encourage applicants to lie on their loan applications to obtain approval for loans they can't possibly afford, sell high-interest loans to borrowers when the borrowers can qualify for low-interest loans, and charge exorbitant mortgage origination fees.

To make loan officers more accountable and clamp down on bad practices, we suggest the following reforms:

- All states should require that all loan officers be licensed. Loan officers typically work for mortgage brokers. Mortgage brokers need to be licensed in all but one state (Alaska), but in many states loan officers are not required to be licensed.
- Loan officers should be required by law to obtain real estate and mortgage fraud training and continuing education in fraud.
- Every loan officer should require careful supervision to provide a system of checks and balances.

Title Companies

A property's deed is a key document in any closing. He who controls the title controls the property and any loans taken out against that property, so con artists often abuse the title and the process for recording deeds in their scams. To wrest control of the title from the con artists, we recommend the following changes to the system:

- Establish a national database in which every title order on a property is recorded immediately.
- Require that every closing must have a title commitment showing all recorded documents within 24 months based on the date of recording, not the document creation date.
- Mandate fraud training for all employees charged with closing loans or disbursing funds.

Protecting the Consumer and the Industry

In recognition of the need for more consistent regulation and supervision of the mortgage lending industry, the Conference of State Bank Supervisors (CSBS) and the American Association of Residential Mortgage Regulators (AARMR) are jointly developing a national licensing system for the residential mortgage industry. The purposes of the system are to enhance consumer protection and streamline the licensing process for regulators and the industry.

The national licensing system will help to protect consumers before they're victimized and aid regulators in supervising mortgage lending and preserve the good names of honest mortgage lenders and brokers. Consumers will have convenient access to key information about the providers of the most important financial transactions of their lives. Through a single website, consumers will be able to ensure they are working with a properly licensed mortgage broker or lender and determine if the licensee has been the subject of any publicly adjudicated enforcement actions.

Some of the system's benefits to consumers, the industry, and regulators include the following:

- Increased accountability of mortgage lenders and brokers (everyone benefits)
- Secure Web access to licensing and enforcement data that are consistent for all state agencies (everyone benefits)
- Submission of a single uniform application or renewal to multiple agencies (industry and regulators benefit)
- Faster approval of new applications, amendments, and renewals (industry and regulators benefit)
- Timely licensing information (contacts, aliases, or doing business as office locations, and so on) that can be updated throughout the year by agencies, lenders, and brokers (everyone benefits)

For more information, visit the CSBS website at *www.csbs.org.*

—*Bill Matthews, Senior Vice President, Conference of State Bank Supervisors*

- Require that lenders use stricter closing instructions regarding the disbursement and diversion of loan funds.
- Establish a mandatory system of checks and balances at every title company.

Builders and Developers

Builders often fall into the trap of providing cash back at closing and other perks to attract new homebuyers rather than simply adjusting the price of a house in relation to current market conditions. To obtain a license, builders should be required to take real estate and mortgage fraud training to learn about these illegal practices.

All licensed builders, superintendents, and managers should be required to take a fraud training course.

Credit Reporting Agencies

Loan officers and lenders typically examine an applicant's credit history prior to approving a loan, but a borrower or someone working on the borrower's behalf can employ all sorts of questionable means to scrub the credit history clean and boost the person's score. To prevent artificially enhanced credit reports from playing a role in loan applications, we suggest the following changes to the system:

- The credit history should be updated and examined 24 hours prior to closing to ensure that the borrower hasn't taken out any last-minute loans that the lender of the current loan is unaware of.
- The credit bureaus need to consider changing their scoring algorithms so that additional cardholder scores are not affected by the length of credit or prior payment history of the primary cardholder.

REO (Real Estate Owned) Brokers

As discussed in chapter 3, unethical REO brokers often sell properties at a discount to their friends, family, and business associates. The lenders who foreclosed on the properties are thus shortchanged out of their rightful revenue, and neighborhood property values are damaged through cut-rate sales. To curb this practice, we recommend the following changes:

- Provide real estate fraud training to all REO brokers.
- Implement random audits of REO broker transactions.
- Create a national database of REO properties so that REO listings are more publicly accessible, or at least encourage lenders to require that all REO properties be listed on the MLS before being sold and that proof of the listing be provided.
- Lenders should hire the appraisers directly rather than relying on the REO broker's appraiser and should not allow any communication between the REO broker and the lender's appraiser.
- Increase civil prosecution against REO brokers who have breached fiduciary duties by failing to represent the interests of their lender clients.

County Recorders

A huge factor contributing to real estate fraud against homeowners is that homeowners are often unaware of any changes to the documents recorded against their homes, including the deed. Another problem is the delay between closing and the recording of the deed, which may enable fraudsters to sell a house multiple times before anyone is aware that the home was already sold. County recorders often rely on antiquated paper systems to record deeds, which can result in delays of six months or more!

To keep homeowners better informed and prevent the delays in recording that con artists often capitalize on, we recommend the following changes at the county level:

- Establish a central database containing the Assessor's Parcel Number or other identification number for every property. Homeowners could register to receive email notification of any changes recorded on their property. People can already do this with their credit reports so the same sort of system should be possible for dealing with property records.
- Every recorder's office should have a system in place that records documents within 24 hours of the time they're filed.
- Property owners should be notified by mail at the property addresses (as well as their last known mailing address) anytime a quitclaim deed is recorded against their property.
- Any incidents of fraud should be reported to a national fraud database.

Attorneys

Not all attorneys are well versed on the subtleties of real estate and mortgage fraud, and consumers should know that. If you're buying or selling a property, always have legal representation from an attorney who practices real estate law. Don't rely on your "family practice" attorney or divorce lawyer for guidance. Just like doctors, attorneys concentrate in different areas. We've been involved in many cases in which attorneys have offered their clients the wrong advice regarding real estate transactions, telling their clients that obviously illegal schemes were okay. Attorneys that give advice in this area need to be educated on lending practices and on the intricacies of mortgage fraud.

ENGAGING IN PRODUCTIVE DISCUSSIONS

We realize that some of the ideas we offer in this chapter on how to reform the system and curb real estate and mortgage fraud are extreme and could be costly, but at the very least they open up areas that are ripe for discussion. Take a moment to consider the amount of money that fraudsters are currently sucking out of the real estate industry through their various scams and schemes—billions of dollars in cash. Charging a nominal fee of $10 for each of the five million or more real estate transactions that close annually could provide sufficient funding to establish a national real estate and mortgage fraud organization to oversee education and reform, or to pay for enhanced law enforcement.

We welcome your input on the ideas and recommendations that we provide in this chapter and encourage you to offer additional suggestions. Simply log on to the Internet, and head to our blogs:

- *FlippingFrenzy.com*
- *MortgageFraudBlog.com*

RESOURCES

Websites

About Ralph Roberts at *aboutralph.com*

Appraisal Buzz at *www.appraisalbuzz.com*

Appraisal Foundation at *www.appraisalfoundation.com*

Appraisal Institute at *www.appraisalinstitute.org*

Appraisal Subcommittee at *www.asc.gov*

Appraisers Forum at *www.appraisersforum.com*

Conference of State Bank Supervisors at *www.csbs.org*

Federal Bureau of Investigation at *www.fbi.gov*

Federal Crimes Blog at *www.federalcrimesblog.com*

Federal Trade Commission at *www.ftc.gov/ftc/consumer.htm*

FlippingFrenzy.com at *www.flippingfrenzy.com*

Freddie Mac's Don't Borrow Trouble at *www.dontborrowtrouble.com*

Georgia Real Estate Fraud Prevention and Awareness Coalition at *www.grefpac.org*

Home Loan Learning Center at *www.homeloanlearningcenter.com*

John T. Reed's Views of Real Estate Investment Gurus at *www.johntreed.com/reedgururating.html*

Matt Norris's Mortgage Cents Blog at *mortgagecents.blogspot.com*

Mortgage Asset Research Institute at *www.mari-inc.com*

Mortgage Bankers Association of America *www.mortgagebankers.org*

Mortgage Fraud Blog at *www.mortgagefraudblog.com*

Mortgage Professor at *www.mtgprofessor.com*

MortgageDaily.com's Fraud Site at *www.mortgagedaily.com/mortgage fraud.asp*

National Mortgage News at *www.nationalmortgagenews.com*

Phil Rice at *mkgappraisal.com/blog/fraud-defined/*

Stop Mortgage Fraud at *www.stopmortgagefraud.com*

U.S. Department of Housing and Urban Development (HUD) at *www.hud.gov*

Publications

"The Detection, Investigation, and Prevention of Insider Loan Fraud: A White Paper," issued May 2003, Federal Financial Institutions Examination Council; *www.ffiec.gov/exam/3P_Mtg_ Fraud_wp_oct04.pdf*

"The Detection, Investigation, and Deterrence of Mortgage Loan Fraud Involving Third Parties: A White Paper," issued February 2005, Federal Financial Institutions Examination Council; *www.ffiec.gov/exam/3P_Mtg_Fraud_wp_oct04.pdf*

"Property Fraud: The Fraud Prevention Role of the Notary Public," Timothy S. Reiniger, Esq., Vice President & Executive Director, National Notary Association (*Title News*, May/June 2005); *www.nationalnotary.org/userimages/prop-fraud1105.pdf*

Combating Fraud and Unethical Practices in Real Estate Transactions, Michael R. Pfeifer, Esq., editor

Detecting and Preventing Real Estate Fraud, Ralph Roberts and Howard Brinton, Star Power; *www.gostarpower.com/shop/prod_detail.asp*

Forensic Accounting and Fraud Investigation for Non-Experts (Hardcover), Howard Silverstone and Michael Sheetz (John Wiley & Sons)

Fraud 101: Techniques and Strategies for Detection, Howard Silverstone and Howard R. Davia (John Wiley & Sons)

Home Insecurity; How Widespread Appraisal Fraud Puts Homeowners at Risk, March 15, 2005, David Callahan, DEMOS; *www.demos. org/pubs/home_insecurity_v3.pdf*

Mortgage Loan Fraud, An Industry Assessment Based upon Suspicious Activity Report Analysis, November 2006; *www.fincen.gov/mortgage loanfraud.pdf*

Predatory Appraisals, Stealing the American Dream, National Community Reinvestment Coalition; *www.ncrc.org/responsible-appraisal/pdfs/ appraisalreport.pdf*

Stealing Home—The Proliferation of Mortgage Fraud, John Jacobs; *www. maddinhauser.com/seminar-materials/05_real_property_seminar/jej.pdf*

The Safety Minute: 01: How to Be Safe in the Streets, at Home, and Abroad So You Can Save Your Life!, Robert Siciliano (Safety Zone Press)

Regulator and Law Enforcement Contacts

Mortgage Fraud Against Lenders at *mbafightsfraud.mortgagebankers. org/reportingfraud.html* provides contact information for the FBI, HUD Field Offices, state attorneys general, each state's real estate commission, and other regulator and law enforcement agencies.

National FBI Financial Institution Fraud Unit

(202) 324-3000

HUD Inspector General

National Hotline
(800) 347-3735

Affinity fraud Any of a number of scams that prey on an identifiable group of people, including minorities or church groups

Air loan Financing that has been approved based entirely or almost entirely on fabrications, including borrowers' identities, title work, pay stubs, bank statements, tax returns, and the appraisal. Sometimes, the house against which the money has been borrowed doesn't even exist.

Asset rental A service that enables borrowers to lease assets, including savings accounts, investments, and real estate, to make the borrowers appear as though they own sufficient collateral to obtain loan approval

Builder bailout Any of several scams a new-construction builder employs to con his way out of a financial fiasco, including submitting fake certifications of work completed to pass inspections, paying off inspectors to approve additional draws from construction loans, selling an unfinished home to a buyer, or using straw buyers as purchasers in order to convert construction financing to permanent financing

Cash back at closing A common type of mortgage fraud in which a buyer agrees to pay more for a house than the seller is asking with the agreement that the seller will kick back the additional money to the buyer, or one of the real estate professionals involved in the transaction, without the lender's knowledge and approval.

Cash back at closing schemes usually involve inflated appraisals. May also be called *cash back after closing.*

Chunking A no-hassle real estate investment scam in which the investor puts up the money, and the con artist promises to do everything else—manage the investment property, find renters, collect rents, and pay the mortgage out of the collected rents—but never delivers on the promise

Credit enhancement Any of several ways people artificially improve their credit history, such as piggybacking on someone else's good credit history. Many companies, particularly on the Internet, offer credit enhancement services.

Deed of trust In certain states, a deed of trust is used instead of a mortgage when a loan is taken out with real property as the collateral. Although foreclosures occur differently under deeds of trust and mortgages, both documents evidence a mortgage debt.

Double-sales scam The practice of selling the same property twice to two different buyers without their knowledge. In counties that have a long delay between closing and the time the deed is recorded, con artists have plenty of time to sell a house two or more times to different buyers.

Equity skimming A type of real estate fraud in which con artists target homeowners who are equity-rich and cash-poor in an attempt to dispossess homeowners of their homes or the equity they have built up in their homes

Flipping The practice of buying a run-down house, improving it cosmetically (if at all), artificially inflating its appraised value, and then selling it quickly for significantly more than its true market value. Sometimes, flippers sell the overpriced home to an unsophisticated buyer. Other times, they work in teams to flip the house several times to one another and then unload it on an unsophisticated buyer or simply obtain the mortgage proceeds and leave the house vacant, allowing it to go to foreclosure.

Foreclosure rescue A type of equity skimming in which so-called investors target homeowners who are facing foreclosure with the promise of "helping" them and then simply help themselves to the home or the equity that the homeowner has built up in the home. Many times these schemes involve the homeowner deeding the title to the home to the rescuer.

Fraud for housing (also known as fraud for property) Any illegal or unethical practice used to gain approval for a mortgage loan that the applicant would not be able to obtain through honest means. Fraud for housing often includes lying about one's employment, obtaining a phony gift letter signed by a relative claiming that the relative has gifted money to cover the down payment, falsifying income or financial records, or having a coapplicant falsely state that she plans on living in the house. In fraud for housing, the borrower actually intends to make the mortgage payments but just can't qualify for the loan without stretching the truth. The main purpose of the fraud is to obtain ownership of the home.

Fraud for profit Any illegal or unethical activity related to a real estate transaction for the purpose of obtaining a profit and where the perpetrators never intend to make the mortgage payments. While homes involved in fraud for housing schemes sometimes end up in foreclosure, those involved in fraud for profit schemes *always* end up in foreclosure. The purpose of the fraud is to line the pockets of the participants.

Identity misrepresentation The use of one or more elements of another person's credit in order to obtain financing; for instance, a son with the same name as his father who uses his father's Social Security number to obtain a loan

Identity theft The stealing of someone's name and personal information. Fraudsters commonly use identity theft to file phony loan applications. See also *professional identity theft.*

Inflated appraisal An official, written estimate of the value of a property claiming that the property is worth more than it really is.

Inflated appraisals are a key component of many types of real estate and mortgage fraud and often contain untruths beyond just the value misrepresentation.

Land sale contract A legal agreement that enables a buyer to purchase a property without having to qualify for a loan. The buyer of the property makes monthly payments directly to the owner but does not obtain title until the purchase price is paid in full. Because most land sale contracts include a forfeiture provision, sellers sometimes use them to repossess a property and keep all of the payments the buyer made simply because the buyer missed a single payment or paid it late.

Lease option A legal agreement in which the seller leases the property to the buyer for a certain period and the buyer has the option to purchase the property. Lease options are often legitimate but can be used by crooked investors to gather payments and then refuse to sell to the buyer at the end of the lease term.

Manufactured housing scam Any of several scams designed to cheat the buyer of a new or used manufactured house, including selling a used house as a new house, failing to deliver the house that the buyer selected, or creating and selling an entire subdivision of homes that lack the required infrastructure (including plumbing and electricity) to make them inhabitable

Mortgage Discharge A document indicating that a mortgage on a house has been paid in full. False Mortgage Discharges are often used in double-sales scams and mortgage elimination schemes. They can often be used to falsely indicate that the previous mortgage on the property has been paid off so the owner (or the person claiming to be the owner) can obtain approval on another loan against the house.

Mortgage elimination A fraudulent scheme in which the con artist attempts to convince homeowners that, under a strict interpretation of the law, they are not obligated to pay off the mortgage on their homes. For a few thousand dollars, the person pitching the mortgage elimination scam offers to file the necessary paperwork to completely eliminate the homeowners' mortgage.

Mortgage fraud Any material misstatement, misrepresentation, or omission of information or supporting documents that a lender or insurer relies on to approve, purchase, or insure a loan

Mortgage satisfaction See also *Mortgage Discharge.*

Ponzi scheme A fraudulent investment scheme in which the con artist sells real estate investments promising unrealistic returns and pays each investor with the proceeds collected from subsequent investors rather than from the return on investment properties, which may or may not exist

Predatory lending Unethical lending practices that harm borrowers. Predatory lending includes charging excessive loan origination fees, packing credit insurance products in loans, and including loan terms that are not disclosed to the borrowers.

Professional identity theft The stealing of a real estate professional's name, license number, and personal information to falsely validate key documents provided at closing, including the title commitment and appraisal

Pyramid scheme A nonsustainable business model that generally doesn't involve the sale of products or services but rather promises that participants will receive payments for enrolling other people in the scheme

Real estate fraud Any criminal or unethical practice or activity intended to deceive, manipulate, or rip off one or more parties involved in a real estate transaction. Real estate fraud includes mortgage fraud. See also *mortgage fraud.*

Reconveyance A document that is recorded when a deed of trust is paid off. See also *Mortgage Discharge.*

Shell company A company set up to receive funds from a fraudulent deal or to launder those funds and that has no legitimate business purpose

Silent second A second mortgage that is not disclosed to the senior lender (the lender who holds the first mortgage). Silent seconds are typically used to disguise the fact that the buyer is not actually making a down payment but is, instead, borrowing the down payment from the seller or another party.

Straw buyer Someone hired or duped into applying for a loan only in name to conceal the identity of the actual loan recipient. Fraudsters often use straw buyers in various real estate and mortgage scams to keep their identities out of the transactions. Also called *straw borrower.*

Straw seller Someone hired to take title to and sell a house only in name to conceal the identity of the actual seller. Fraudsters often use straw sellers as intermediaries in real estate and mortgage scams so that they can buy and quickly resell properties without having their names appear in the chain of title.

Tax deed A document that transfers ownership of a property from the homeowners who failed to pay their property taxes to an investor who purchased the tax deed at auction. Phony tax deeds are often used to convince homeowners that the person holding the deed is the legal owner of the property.

Tax lien certificate A document that transfers the right to collect on back property taxes from the taxing authority to an investor. Con artists may present a tax lien certificate to homeowners who have fallen behind on their taxes as proof that the con artist now is the legal owner of the property, even though the homeowners may still have legal rights to pay the back taxes and interest and retain possession of the property.